Advance Praise for

BOOMER REINVENTION

"John Tarnoff is a beacon for anyone looking for a fresh approach to living life's second half with meaning, purpose and impact. This is a book that should be used and re-used, so keep it on a low shelf of your book case!"

> —Marci Alboher, VP Encore.org, and author of *The Encore Career Handbook: How to Make a Living and a Difference in the Second Half of Life.*

"Just stop thinking that your career is (almost) over when you hit your 50s. Despite ageism, downsizing, and the rest of the post-digital indignities (retirement savings, anyone?), John Tarnoff paints an empowering picture of what we can all do to stay sane, solvent, and sustainable in this next stage of life and career."

> —Lisa Birnbach, author of The Official Preppy Handbook, and True Prep; Vanity Fair and The New Yorker contributor

"*Boomer Reinvention* is a candid and accurate portrayal of the current job market and the boomer reality. It's a great, realistic, and practical guide that addresses the psychology of change (which is often overlooked), uncertainty, and even failure, while providing encouragement, hope, and even a bit of humor."

> —Terry Bradwell, EVP & Chief Enterprise Strategy and Innovation Officer at AARP

"This is a wonderful thoughtful book, not just a life preserver thrown into choppy waters, but a practical set of new perspectives to assume, and the most important new steps to take, to begin the great and honorable American tradition of reinvention. It's never too late and things are never so bad that a new chapter can't begin. Now, here's the toolbox--joyously useful and hugely indispensable."

> —Ken Burns, filmmaker

"Boomers have many available resources when it comes to reinventing their careers, but *Boomer Reinvention* goes the extra mile by creating a smart, modular approach that will benefit you, no matter what your personal or professional aspirations."

> —Nancy Collamer, career consultant, speaker, Forbes and US News contributor; author of *Second-Act Careers: 50+ Ways to Profit from Your Passions During SemiRetirement*

"*Boomer Reinvention* is an absolute must for anyone who is navigating a career change. John Tarnoff lovingly helps readers tap into their own life experiences, by embracing both successes and failures, to envision and pursue exciting new professional pathways. This handy guidebook is packed with inspiring real-life stories, a practical 5-step plan, and a vote of confidence that creating a meaningful second act is possible."

> —Catherine Collinson, Nationally recognized retirement expert, thought leader, researcher and advocate

"John Tarnoff is a master of reinvention and masters the subject for the rest of us in this terrific book. Anyone over 50 who is thinking about What If? and How Can I? will find Boomer Reinvention a valuable and entertaining resource, stuffed with plenty of practical advice."

—Richard Eisenberg, Work & Purpose Editor, Nextavenue.org

"Transitions are often harder than we expect, or hope. John Tarnoff's five-step approach is an incredibly useful blueprint for navigating this exciting stage of life."

—Chris Farrell, Senior Economics Contributor, Marketplace, Author of *Unretirement*

"What we used to think of as "retirement" has flipped into an entirely new, active and productive life stage. John Tarnoff brilliantly unravels the personal journey necessary to take full advantage of this opportunity, and provides a compelling—and beautifully written--roadmap to reaping the rewards of an encore career."

—Marc Freedman, Founder/CEO, Encore.org, author of *The Big Shift*

"For most of us, traditional 'retirement' retired before we got a chance to try it. Reinvention has become our new necessity of life. John Tarnoff not only lives reinvention, he's written us an elegant and practical user's guide."

—Hon. Josh Gotbaum, former banker, Treasury official, & pension guarantor, reinvented in the Brookings Institution Retirement Security Project.

"Skip the Botox, get a faith lift! Career coach John Tarnoff has written a spirited, practical and can-do new book, skillfully showing readers how to take back control of their careers in his step-by-step methodology."

—Kerry Hannon, author of *Getting the Job You Want After 50 and Love Your Job, The New Rules for Career Happiness*

"As John Tarnoff shows, the makings of your second act — one filled with meaning and purpose — are already there. And with this inspiring and yet very practical book, he gives us a step by step guide in how to tap into it."

—Arianna Huffington, CEO and Founder of Thrive Global

"Our 50s (and beyond) have the potential to be the most fulfilling years in our careers and lives. John Tarnoff's *Boomer Reinvention* shows how we can align our innate wisdom and creativity with our skills and abilities, and create a sustainable bright future living with purpose and meaning."

—Agapi Stassinopoulos , Author, *Wake Up to the Joy of You: 52 Meditations and Practices for a Calmer, Happier Life*

BOOMER
REINVENTION

BOOMER
REINVENTION

How to Create Your Dream Career Over 50

JOHN TARNOFF

REINVENTION PRESS

Los Angeles

Library of Congress Control Number: 2016958263 Paperback ISBN 978-0-9979539-0-9 e-book ISBN 978-0-9979539-1-6

website: www.boomerreinvention.com
twitter: @johntarnoff
facebook: www.facebook.com/boomerreinvention

First Edition

Published in the United States of America

To Dorothy
the original career reinventor

"Lately it occurs to me
What a long, strange trip it's been."
—The Grateful Dead
Truckin'

CONTENTS

ACKNOWLEDGMENTS

THIS ALL STARTED ONE DAY in 2012 when I got a call from Sandy VandenBerge, who was then V.P. at the Long Beach Community Foundation. She was inviting me to speak at her upcoming TEDx event, TEDx SoCal. The theme was "**The Alchemy of Transformation...Our Selves, Our Work Places, Our Living Spaces,**" and I assumed she was interested in hearing me talk about the digital disruptions that have taken place in the media/entertainment business. Previously, I had keynoted a conference that the Foundation had sponsored on transforming the City of Long Beach into a more digitally-oriented creative hub, so this seemed a logical extension of that topic. But Sandy told me I could speak about whatever I chose, and for some strange reason that I still can't quite explain, I decided that what I really wanted to talk about was the career challenge facing the baby boomer generation, and how we needed to transform ourselves in this new post-recession economy.

That spark has led me on quite a journey over the past almost five years. While I got great responses to my TEDx talk, it took me another year or so to finally figure out that this was actually a career direction that I wanted to pursue. Arianna Huffington and her sister Agapi Stassinopoulos had been encouraging me to blog on the Huffington Post, and I realized that I finally had a topic. With the support of Senior Editor Shelley Emling, I researched and wrote a series of posts about boomers who had reinvented themselves. This research brought me in touch with fellow boomers across a range of backgrounds and career pursuits. As I deepened my familiarity and understanding of this topic, it became clear that the next step was to take what I had learned through my research and my interviews, and combine that with the five-step methodology I had outlined in my TEDx talk, and... write this book.

Now, almost two years later, it's quite amazing to look back and take stock of the enthusiasm and support that I have received from so many people in putting this project together and getting it out the door.

I suppose it always starts with a big and messy first draft, and John Eggen and Jill Cheeks coached me through it, and helped me hit my milestones. I also received encouragement from my new friends in the encore career community, including Marc Freedman, Marci Alboher, Nancy Collamer, Richard Eisenberg, Chris Farrell and Kerry Hannon, all of whom welcomed this unknown acolyte into their midst.

Phil Glosserman, Ellen Sherman, Kimberly Cameron and Anne Yeager gave me some very early and helpful feedback. In retrospect, they were much too polite, but maybe somehow magically also saw its potential. Allen Rinzler and I had a brief but meaningful exchange that helped dissipate some of the fogginess around the first draft, and wound up setting the stage for what became a very effective collaboration with my editor, Karl Weber. Karl and I first sat down over coffee at the Grand Hyatt in New York and he told me: "You have four different books here. Which one do you actually want to write?" In the ensuing months, Karl helped me reshape what I had written, and concentrate on the practical prescription that I hope makes the book stand out. Karl also encouraged me to seek out and incorporate the reinvention experiences of the seven boomers I was able to contact and profile for these pages. I am indebted to these collaborators, David Beadle, Judy Contreras, Marilyn Friedman, Dan Goetz, Julie Murphy, John Pugliano, and Valerie Ramsay, and thank them for their willingness to risk sharing their time and experiences with me – expecting but not knowing whether their stories would ever actually make it into print.

So much of this book, and my approach to coaching, has been inspired and shaped by my University of Santa Monica experience, and by the wise and thoughtful curriculum devised by Drs. Ron and Mary Hulnick - who will find their influence very apparent throughout these pages. As I struggled to stay focused over the past two years, my fellow USM adjunct faculty colleagues and leadership (you know who you are), provided perhaps the most consistent and persistent (and joyful) support imaginable.

Coming down the final stretch, Richard Kletter, Adam Leipzig, and Kevin Stein have been valued and consistent consiglieris. One of life's more amazing experiences is the freshness and consistency of longstanding friendships, as represented by my Amherst College mafia, Mark Gerchick, Peter Scheer, Charlie Trueheart, and Bill Woolverton. They have been the cheering section every career re-inventor would be lucky to have. My launch team has been a gift – a collection of talented individuals who helped me put this book into your hands (or onto your screen): Adil Dara, Glen Edelstein, Jessica Gould and the indefatigable Courtney Greenhalgh.

Acknowledgments would not be complete without a special shout-out to Dan Green, my partner-in-crime at Carnegie Mellon's Los Angeles-based Entertainment Industry Management graduate program. Dan has been with me from the beginning on this, coaching me on that TEDx talk, and being super accommodating in helping me juggle my new and ever increasing preoccupation with the "boomer thing" with my no-less fascinating and absorbing day job.

Finally, I couldn't have completed the book without the two most consistent day-to-day influences in my life: my daughter Jessy, whose presence reminds me every day what life is all about (no, really), and the amazing Deana Marconi, whose unconditional love and partnership have helped sustain and grow my own reinvention.

Introduction

IS THIS BOOK FOR YOU?

I DON'T KNOW ABOUT YOU, but I can't really afford to retire. Not anytime soon, anyway. Yes, I have some retirement savings—what's left over from the devastation of the Great Recession—but not enough to maintain anywhere near the lifestyle I'm currently living, restrained and sensible as it may be.

Lots of us baby boomers (born between 1946 and 1964) are in the same boat. Since the recession decimated up to half the value of our homes, our savings accounts, and our 401(k)s, we boomers have woken up to the new reality about retirement in the twenty-first century. Retirement as we expected it is pretty much over. A relatively small number of us (between 5 and 15 percent, depending on which surveys you read) have either saved enough, or will be provided with enough of a pension, to sustain our current lifestyles beyond the traditional retirement age of sixty-five. That's between four and eleven million people out of the seventy-two million boomers still walking around in the United States. As for the rest of us— well, we've got a problem on our hands.

The fact is that the world we've inherited is a far different world from the one that we were promised. We grew up in an age when corporate America was on the ascendant, and the compact between the corporation and the employee was a two-way street. We believed that the corporation we went to work for after graduating would train us, promote us, and give us a fat pension and a gold watch for our retirement. But the world has changed. Corporate loyalty to employees is a thing of the past.

For many boomers who were lucky enough to hold onto their jobs for two or even three decades, large-scale reorganizations, downsizing, and early retirement buyouts have left us feeling betrayed and adrift. Even if we are still getting a paycheck, more and more of us belong to a segment of the workforce a friend of mine has dubbed "the working worried"— those wondering whether today is the day they're going to receive their pink slip.

As a result, many people feel awkward, afraid, and ashamed of where they find themselves in their fifties: insecure or undervalued in their jobs, having suffered downsizing for no good reason, financially unprepared for retirement, and unwilling to accept that their working lives are just being tossed aside. We are angry—justifiably—that in many cases our careers are being cut short while we are still arguably at the top of our game.

Economic trends are part of the problem. But simple bias is another. Yes, ageism is a fact of life in our culture. Maybe it's a holdover from industrial society, which rounded up everyone over sixty-five and stashed them away to wait to die when they only had a few years left in any event. Maybe it's an outgrowth of our obsession with novelty, which makes us label anything old as outmoded, irrelevant, boring. Whatever the reasons, we need a counter-narrative to the assumption that being over sixty-five means that you have nothing left to contribute, that you're somehow out of touch, that your skills are outdated, and that your experience means nothing.

Perhaps most painful is acknowledging that we, too, are part of the problem. Many boomers are held by our own unwillingness to change and adapt to the world around us. Many of us have in fact outgrown the jobs and careers we have, and lingering in these stagnant situations can make us turn brittle and bitter. There's a good chance that the malaise you're feeling at work reflects not just your uncertain future prospects but some deeper longing that is driven from within. You may be ready for a change that fulfills your need for meaning and purpose, to leave a legacy, or simply to no longer march to someone else's drumbeat.

Career reinvention, then, is really an imperative for anyone who has any uncertainty about their long-term financial, emotional, and physical health. We have to do everything we can to prolong our ability to provide for ourselves, contribute our wisdom and experience to society, and leave a meaningful legacy.

A DIFFERENT TAKE

This book offers a practical prescription for boomers to take back control of their careers. It is based on one key paradigm and one key assumption.

The key paradigm: reinvention is not about trying to figure out what job or business you can fit into out there. It's about figuring out what job or business is *already inside you*, aching to come out and play, and then taking the necessary steps to make it a reality.

The key assumption: in order to create the future, you have to resolve the past. There is no use in pivoting to a new job or a new calling—or even in renewing or reformulating the job you already have—unless you first deal with all the old baggage and self-limitations that are likely standing in your way.

Boomer Reinvention is a five-step framework that includes twenty-three separate strategies—personal and career development tools to conceive, plan, and implement a better, more autonomous, more resonant, and more resilient career that you can pursue for many years to come. It can provide you with an ongoing foundation for overcoming the obstacles and uncertainties associated with career change. I invite you to visit the associated website www.boomerreinvention.com, where I've posted all of the worksheets you'll find in this book.

Career reinvention is not about following a cookie-cutter job-seeking prescription. It's about creating your own formula based on your own reflection, your own research, and your own focus on what has worked for you in the past, what motivates you and excites you in the present, and what could sustain and gratify you in the future.

WE STILL HAVE TIME

We boomers are getting to that stage in life when funerals and memorial services are becoming the new ritual gatherings that weddings and baby showers once occupied in our social calendars. It's unpleasant to realize that friends and family members are beginning to die around us. But it brings up an all-important question: How do you want to live out the rest of your life? Isn't it time to address that bucket list, starting with the work that you could be doing every day?

And many of us have a lot of years to look forward to. According to the Social Security Administration, 25 percent of us who live past sixty-five are going to live past ninety. We're already seeing how medical advances have prolonged the lives of our parents. Just think what continued progress will mean for us.

But the opportunity to live longer lives also brings serious challenges. We have to come to terms with the fact that we can't take the future for granted, and assume that things are going to somehow magically "work out." We have to develop a realistic plan for economic survival that can sustain us for twenty-five, even thirty-five years beyond the traditional retirement age. At the same time, the perspective that age and experience bring will also likely cause you to reevaluate and recalibrate your career in terms of how you're feeding your soul, not just how you're feeding your bank account.

One of the boomers I've interviewed for my *Huffington Post* series on reinvented boomers was a man who ran a paper mill for many years, and was actually succeeding in keeping the company profitable despite the massive digital disruption of the paper industry. But his adult son kept urging him to look at the legacy he was leaving, and challenging him about whether he wanted to "die as a net polluter." So this guy took early retirement, left the paper industry, and opened up a franchise business selling renewable energy products to small businesses and consumers. Like many boomers, he embraced a new attitude about life and work.

HOW I GOT HERE

I'm not a traditional career counselor. I'm actually a guy who's been fired a lot. Like you, I have been, over the years, trying to figure out how to have a meaningful, purposeful career in what was for me a very tumultuous but fascinating creative business. So I have learned about Boomer Reinvention by doing it, by trying and failing, and picking myself up and trying again.

If you look up the word "peripatetic" in the dictionary, you might just find my name listed next to it. For most of the past forty years, I have worked as an executive in the Hollywood entertainment business, along with stints as a film producer and tech entrepreneur during the 1990s "bubble." Hollywood careers are notoriously volatile, and I guess I have had what some people would characterize as a rich and diverse set of work experiences (but which my late mother might have lamented as simply my inability or unwillingness to hold a job).

In fact, in doing the math on the eighteen jobs I held over the thirty-five years preceding my current work as a university educator and career coach, I was fired from seven of them, which means that I've been fired 39 percent of the time in my career. I joked about this in a TEDx talk in 2012 where I introduced the five Boomer Reinvention steps, and it has since become something of a trademark for me. But the point of talking about it is to destigmatize the idea of getting fired. It's time to stop feeling that having been fired or downsized is somehow shameful. At this point in our lives, I think we have to just chalk this stuff up, wear our battle scars proudly, have a sense of humor about our misfortunes, and be grateful for the lessons. We're still standing!

Having gotten fired from 39 percent of my jobs has given me some specific insights into how you can recover from a career setback, work through it, and even use it to your advantage.

My watershed career reinvention happened when I was fifty. The tech startup that I had cofounded had gone belly-up (along with most of the other early dotcom ventures). I had lost traction with my old Hollywood circles and had no idea where to go or what to do. So I went back to school to earn a psychology degree, thinking that I might learn something about what made me tick and that I could pick up some tools that would help me move on to something new. As it turned out, I was pulled back into the entertainment business, working for DreamWorks Animation, but in a completely new role—working on people-oriented initiatives to develop internal artistic training programs, and to foster relationships with colleges and universities to recruit entry-level talent. I found this transition to education and training completely inspiring, and when I got to the end of the line with DreamWorks in 2009, I was determined to continue on the same vector. I now co-run a Los Angeles–based graduate program in Entertainment Management for Carnegie Mellon University and coach my fellow boomers on reinventing their careers. Hence this book.

Going forward, my plan is to work as long as I can—beyond seventy when my social security benefit maxes out, and at least until seventy-five. I hope to shore up my savings and increase the odds that I'll be able to sustain myself into my eighties or beyond. If I'm lucky, I'll end up like my stepfather, who came home one evening from a good day at the office, went out to dinner with my mother and some friends, and simply didn't wake up the following morning. He was ninety.

HOW TO USE THIS BOOK

This book is part manifesto, part workbook. In Part I, I summarize the changes that have happened all around us and the resulting dangers and challenges that await us, and suggest some reasons why you should consider reinventing your career before that reinvention is forced on you by external circumstances.

Today's business climate is vastly different from the one we boomers started out in. The digital revolution has increased the pace of change remarkably, and that has led to changes in the way we hire and get hired in a much flatter, more team-oriented business hierarchy. It has also underscored the need for us to continue to learn, to train and to expand our skill sets to stay up to speed with change, and to be more open and more transparent in the way we represent ourselves.

Reinventing your career means shifting your mindset as well as your job description. You're entering a new career stage where you'll get a chance to use everything you've learned in a new way. What's more, the context of your second-act career is new. Rather than working to make money, support a family, and achieve personal or lifestyle goals, your second-act career is the opportunity to also create meaning and purpose, to leave a legacy, and to be of service. It's a different way of going into work in the morning, and a pretty inspiring way to live.

In Part II, I profile a set of boomers who exemplify the career reinvention process. Their personal journeys illustrate the kinds of transformations that we all can make to get our careers turned around and pointed in a positive direction. While each of them went about their reinvention in a different way, they all share the key attitudes and practices that I've synthesized in the Boomer Reinvention methodology.

Part III, the heart of the book, walks you through the five Boomer Reinvention steps. It provides a set of training materials you can use to fuel and support your career turnaround. I developed the Boomer Reinvention methodology while blundering through my own repeated job changes and career reinventions. It draws on both my business experiences over the course of my forty-year career and the studies in behavioral and spiritual psychology that culminated in my MA degree from the University of Santa Monica graduate program in 2005. Using these tools will help you approach your quest for a sustainable career with a lot more certainty, a lot more confidence in yourself, and a greater sense of opportunity and expansiveness.

OUTER EXPERIENCE IS A REFLECTION OF INNER REALITY

Career reinvention takes hard work. It won't happen overnight or over a weekend. Your mileage may vary, depending on your willingness to engage fully with your program. But if you spend time road-testing these five steps and twenty-three strategies, you will be a lot closer to landing a new job or career that will sustain you as long as you are motivated and able to work.

The purpose of this book is to help you shift your consciousness from depending on the outside world for your career epiphany to cultivating and relying on your own inner knowledge to make you strong and resolute in your reinvention. It is an opportunity to take a deep dive into the heart of what makes you tick, and what inspires you to do and be your best. It is a chance for you to take stock of your last thirty or forty years and create a plan you can feel excited about and committed to every morning.

No one else is going to figure it out for you. Railing against the injustices of corporate downsizing, ageism, or any other reason for your current vulnerability isn't going to help you. The only way forward for each one of us is to take charge of our own careers, find the niche that best represents our usefulness to the world—and just go for it.

If you're still reading, then you'll likely enjoy the rest.

Part I

THE REINVENTION IMPERATIVE

Chapter 1

WAKING UP TO A NEW REALITY

BOOMERS ARE, AND WILL CONTINUE TO BE, excellent choices for today's and tomorrow's workforce. But for the moment, the message from the top to the bottom of the American enterprise is that older workers need to be weaned out before they hit sixty-five. The ingrained assumption is that older workers are just supposed to "move over" because they offer no obvious benefit to employers or to the economy at large. Many employers hide behind the shibboleths about the propensity of injury, elevated healthcare costs for older workers (who can actually rely on Medicare), and the idea that older workers won't stay at the job for long. The truth is that older workers are no different from younger workers in these areas, and may even be more reliable and more focused on their jobs because they are older. With families grown and life's lessons behind them, they are likely to be less distracted, more appreciative of the work, and more dependable.

Age bias is being increasingly discussed in the media, and while there is still much work to do, business leaders are beginning to recognize the special value we boomers can provide. Some companies, for example, are instituting "phased retirement" plans, where employees stay in their jobs, reduce their hours, and engage in more mentoring, knowledge transfer, and staff development while developing new career opportunities for themselves beyond their companies. This allows for a smoother transition into a second-act career and is a smart way to take advantage of the wisdom and experience that these often lifelong employees can provide.

But these changes are slow to materialize for most of us in the workforce, and if we are going to prolong our careers, we are going to need a clearer understanding of some of the ways that the career marketplace has changed over the last twenty years while we were just minding our business and doing our jobs.

Boomers have an opportunity to get more comfortable with change, even to make change our friend. That is going to make us a whole lot more competitive as a generation, will open up channels of communication and understanding with younger people, and will allow us to emerge as new leaders and co-creators of our future.

Here are four of the big changes in the career marketplace you are likely to encounter as you embark on your personal reinvention process.

DIGITAL IS NOT A PROBLEM

It's a cliché, but the digital revolution did indeed change everything. And the breadth of these changes poses a career challenge for many of us raised in an analog age.

The irony of the digital revolution is that we boomers invented it. I find it funny when younger people talk about the digital skills gap, and how "digital natives" who grew up with technology have a significant advantage over older workers. But Steve Jobs, Bill Gates, Jeff Bezos, Tim Berners-Lee (who invented the World Wide Web), and many more internet visionaries are or were boomers. The global infrastructure that has enabled the massive disruption of pretty much every traditional business process on the planet was all patched together by a cadre of boomer (and older) engineers and entrepreneurs over the last forty years. So while our kids may be "digital natives," I like to think of us as "digital founders."

But some of us have indeed been slow to surrender the old paradigms we grew up with. Digital has obviously accelerated the pace of change. But for us to understand, if not embrace, that acceleration, we have to be mindful of the way software works and drop any lingering resistance to the always-on, massively collaborative, open, flat, and transparent world we are living in. As digital founders, we have the insight and perspective that comes from understanding the advantages as well as the limitations of the digital world. I don't think the problem is that we are somehow ignorant or incapable (as a generation) of understanding technology; we just have a longer memory and can see both sides of this equation. By getting up to speed and staying up to date, we can use digital tools to thoroughly empower our second-act careers. We were the generation that insisted on doing our homework while listening to the radio and talking on the phone. I think we can handle the wizardry of a connected world.

YOUR RÉSUMÉ WON'T GET YOU HIRED

When we lose a job, the first move we're supposed to make is to dig out our résumé (if we can find it), stick a fresh sheet of paper into the typewriter, and give it an update—a process that many people find excruciating. Ironically, in the digital age, your résumé is no longer the primary job-getting tool it once was. Back in the days of snail mail and faxes, the hiring cycle was analog, slower, and much more genteel.

What's worse, chasing job openings on the internet turns out to be a fool's game. The biggest job-hunting mistake you can make, particularly at our age, is to try to identify jobs through job postings you read online, and to then submit a résumé and a cover letter to the email address associated with that job posting.

First, think of how many people are likely competing with you for that job. The scale and reach of the internet gives employers unprecedented access to job candidates. The average corporate job posting gets 250 résumé submissions—and the first one arrives within three minutes of it being posted. Over 425,000 résumés are posted each *week* on Monster.com, most of them shotgunned across multiple open positions on multiple websites.

As a result, most recruiters are completely overwhelmed by the volume of applications they receive. And because it is so easy to apply for a job online, there is a strong likelihood that the vast majority of applications do not qualify for a given opening. So the recruiter or their staff will be assuming—rightly so—that most of the *résumés* they're receiving won't measure up. In the old days, a recruiter might have spent thirty seconds skimming your résumé to see if you had the right mix of skills and experience for the job. Today, that recruiter spends about seven seconds on your résumé. If nothing sticks out, you quickly wind up in what we used to refer to (before the Delete key) as the "circular file." Is it any wonder that so many people—particularly boomers—complain about never hearing back from recruiters to whom they've submitted résumés and job applications?

Here's another reason why relying on your résumé is a mistake: hiring managers are looking elsewhere for viable candidates. In fact, only 15 percent of job openings are filled from online applications. The majority of jobs are filled internally or through referrals.

Hiring has become a lot more decentralized as companies are evolving beyond rigid hierarchies and relying on small teams working within flatter organizational structures. Teams are now increasingly responsible for hiring their teammates. For example, each department at your nearest Whole Foods Market manages its own P&L and is responsible for its own hiring practices, as well as its own inventory management, customer relations, and bottom line.

So most hiring managers today are going to want to reach out to their established business networks to fill their open positions. They're going to want to meet people through referrals from friends and colleagues whose judgment they trust and who can refer likeminded people who will be a better fit for an open position.

Conclusion: your résumé doesn't get you in the door. Certainly, it is a valuable record of your accomplishments. A well-organized, readable, and properly-drafted résumé is a great asset *after* you have gotten your foot in the door and had an interview. At that point, your *r*ésumé becomes the script that an enthusiastic recruiter or hiring manager will use to promote you and explain your value to the rest of their team and to the higher-ups who are going to have to approve their decision to hire you.

LEARNING IS LIFELONG

Many boomers grew up believing that our degrees and diplomas entitled us to employment. In our parents' generation, you could live out your entire career with a high school diploma as a blue-collar worker or with a BA degree as a white-collar worker. Professionals with advanced degrees—the lawyers, doctors, and accountants—could coast as well. So the idea was simple: front-load your education in your teens and twenties, endure a backbreaking apprenticeship, and then sail through to retirement.

That is no longer the way it works. As a university educator, I've seen that the BA is the new high school diploma and the master's degree is the new BA. In a more complex, more changeable world, employers seeking to fill entry-level positions are looking for kids who have more years of schooling and domain-specific training under their belt. Just imagine how they've raised the bar for us boomers!

In this new world, adapting to change and learning new skills are crucial. If you've been in a job for the last ten or fifteen years, you've likely had to do a certain amount of training or professional development, but this can no longer be seen as a nice add-on to your core training and background. You have to look at training as an ongoing proposition if you're going to be competitive with the rest of the workforce.

Ultimately, your ability is your new credential. Your ability to get something done is more important than the degree you got twenty or thirty years ago. You need to see your résumé less as a listing of traditional credentials and more as an artist's portfolio, where each position you've held, each project you've been responsible for, and each challenge you've successfully overcome becomes a story point in an overall narrative of your career. You need to demonstrate how your portfolio of skills, experiences, and growth opportunities makes you the perfect fit for the job you're trying to get, the consulting contract you're pitching, or the new business for which you're seeking investment funds.

DELIVERING VALUE, NOT TIME

It is no longer OK to just show up on time and punch the clock, thinking that what you did yesterday or how you did it justifies your continued employment in today's or tomorrow's world. That's the old industrial model. In today's postindustrial world, you have to be willing to make new stuff, adopt new ideas, and engage more proactively in creating value. Value can take many forms—productivity, intellectual property, profitability, innovation, service, creativity—but in a postindustrial knowledge economy, it is up to you to understand what that value is for the customer, client, or company you're working for, and then to overdeliver on that value.

It doesn't matter what kind of job you're doing; whether you're working as an independent contractor on a 1099 or as a salaried worker on a W2, you have to think of yourself as a consultant delivering value to a client rather than an employee working under the direction of a supervisor. It is no longer enough to ask to be assigned a task. Anyone can execute (and that "anyone" is going to be younger and cheaper than you are). You need to stay as many steps ahead of the game as you can, probe deeply into the unknown, anticipate where that value is, and learn how to deliver it.

Smart professionals have already started reorganizing their work lives around these principles. A few years ago, a group of accountants around the country got together to change the way they performed services and provided value to their clients. The call themselves Cliff Jumpers. They stopped billing by the hour, and, instead, decided to provide a unique set of services to niche clients with specific needs, including many startup businesses whose accounting needs couldn't be quantified by hourly billing. Instead, these accountants began providing more strategic, "noncommodity," forward-thinking analyses to help their clients plan for the future and economize in the present. They negotiated their fees based not on how many hours they had worked for the client, but on how much money they had both saved and made for the client as a result of their work.

The Cliff Jumpers represent the kind of value-based thinking that is going to be increasingly necessary—both to deal with the complexities of business today, but also as a way to stand out and be different from the competition.

As you can see, these four big changes in the workplace—the digital revolution, the decline of the résumé, the need for lifelong learning, and the shift from delivering time to delivering value—have redefined the way careers take shape in today's world. They provide the background against which your reinvention process will take place.

Chapter 2

EMBRACING YOUR
SECOND ACT

SINCE I BEGAN COACHING BOOMERS on figuring out how to prolong their careers, I see more and more people just simply blowing past the idea of retirement. Maybe we need to redefine it as "Re-engagement" or "Re-fire-ment," or "Returnment" or any number of similar alternative labels that bloggers and pundits have come up with. Clearly the folks at AARP, led by the dynamic JoAnn Jenkins, are rebranding themselves not simply as a resource for retirement, but as a broad set of work and lifestyle solutions for everyone over fifty. Their "Disrupt Aging" slogan is a call to action aimed across all generations to rethink the outdated biases that marginalize older workers, but that also disadvantage and send the wrong signals to younger workers. In the end, their goal is to achieve a truly multi-generational culture and workforce. Another visionary, Marc Freedman, and his nonprofit Encore.org have built an organization and a movement around the idea of an encore career that matches up engaged aspiring social entrepreneurs over sixty with causes and opportunities to give back and make a difference.

Many of us are overcoming the challenges of traversing our careers at this stage. We're opening businesses, going back to school, and generally dusting ourselves off because we have to figure out how to keep going. Many empty-nesters are open to downsizing our lives and even working for less money in jobs that are more rewarding. We're searching for ways to live more in line with who we are and what we want to do at this stage in our lives—and continue to make money while we do it. We may not all be working forty-hour weeks, but it seems pretty clear that we are all going to have to keep working as long as we possibly can in today's and tomorrow's economy.

Our parents were winding down at this point—and the rest of the world, reflexively, has been expecting us to do the same. But most baby boomers both want and need to keep working and keep going. We're trying to figure out a new way to engage with the world in the midst of an emerging, unprecedented life stage that defies categorization. It is not simply an extension of our careers—it really is a Second Act.

WHAT IS REINVENTION?

Reinvention is the process that gets us to that second act in our work lives. It is not an end in itself. It is a means to a better, more effective, more rewarding life and career. It is not an event but a process. The point is not to announce to your friends that you have reinvented yourself. The point is to be able to make confident decisions about what you want to do with your life and career—decisions that are heartfelt, authentic, and deeply rooted in who you are.

Reinvention is about manifesting something out in the world and changing your career, and, by extension, your life. Reinvention implies a deep willingness to surrender the old ways that you used to live and work. It is reinvigorating, inspiring, and energizing.

Reinvention is an iterative process. It requires a certain amount of tearing everything down from the past in order to start from scratch. It involves questioning assumptions, getting feedback, taking a good long look in the mirror, being okay with yourself, and slogging through the various possibilities of what's right for you, often hitting a dead end or making a wrong decision until you come up with the right formula. Just like an inventor.

Reinvention has become a bit of a cliché in the media, where the term is bandied about loosely to describe any kind of inspiring personal or professional change. People who reinvent themselves are touted as the pioneers, the outliers, the special ones. They're uniquely resourceful, disciplined, visionary, fearless, and confident. Described in this way, reinvention sounds very intimidating. As the media pundits would have it, only the special among us can actually pull it off.

But while reinvention is not for the faint of heart, it is attainable and workable for anyone who is willing to engage with the process and walk the walk.

You don't have to turn your life upside down to reinvent your career. You can even reinvent your *current* job if you're willing and able to devise a way to provide greater value in a more updated and relevant way.

Reinvention means that an epiphany has taken place. It means that you have looked deeply at who you are, what you do, and what you can do, and have made a conscious and informed choice to shift your work in a new direction with a new outlook and a new understanding.

Reinvention represents a willingness to challenge your comfort zone every day, and to change your focus from preserving security to accepting change. It represents an openness and a willingness to consider or experience risk that you may not have allowed yourself to experience up until now.

One of the reinvented boomers I profiled for my Huffington Post blog is a guy named Jim Milligan, a 3M executive in Michigan who planned his retirement as if it were an entrepreneurial launch. Milligan was inspired by a trip to Italy to create a retail business devoted to fine olive oils. With no prior retail or importing experience, he built a business from the ground up that has become quite successful. I call him the Howard Schultz of olive oil because his story echoes the way Schultz was inspired by the coffee bars of Italy to create his iconic Starbucks chain.

Another profile was of boomer fashion designer Marla Wynne Ginzberg, a television producer whose career and marriage blew up. Without any special training or background, Ginzberg decided there was an empty niche in fashion design for boomer women like her. She cut and sewed her first clothing line at home, pounded pavement and networked her way to find backing and distribution, and has been successfully building her brand online, on TV shopping channels, and in retail.

THE NEW LEADERSHIP CRITERIA

When you were young, you may have been frustrated in your job searches by the fact that you didn't have the experience that recruiters were looking for. Now that you are a veteran of the workplace, it's cruelly ironic that, in today's world, experience is no longer viewed as the magic key to success. The view today is that leading through turbulent times is not necessarily helped by our experience, because today's challenges may be too new, and outside the realm of that experience. In times of radical change like these, we need to be able to navigate without a net, and without necessarily referencing the past.

For this reason, staffing executives now regard what they call your "potential," plus your personal qualities and your character traits, as crucial to measuring your leadership abilities. Fortunately, there's a good chance that you will find that many of the markers that companies now seek in candidates are ones you've developed over the years through the ups and downs of your career. Here are six of the traits that hiring managers and academics have identified as keys to success in today's workplace—particularly for those who are leaders in organizations.

A Service Attitude

Being of service means that you are thinking about the team of people you work with before you think about yourself. Leaders who employ an attitude of service see themselves primarily as facilitators and mediators who are there to remove obstacles preventing people from doing the work they were hired to do. The attitude might be summed up by the old adage "Hire the best people, and then let them do their job." More than just macro-managers, service-oriented leaders are attuned to personalities and finding ways of promoting harmony and collaboration. While plan-driven or authoritarian leaders will be looking over their shoulder, making sure that everyone is following them, service-oriented leaders are more like shepherds herding the flock. Service-oriented leaders follow their people, always facing forward, scanning farther ahead, and making sure that everyone is included and going in the right direction.

Long-Term Vision

The leader with potential must always evaluate the long-term consequences of today's decisions and directions. This flies in the face of the widespread business emphasis on "making the quarter" and focusing on short-term tactical targets. Focusing on the long term requires the creativity and imagination to weigh multiple potential outcomes, and the courage to make decisions that may not immediately make sense to those who are only looking a few steps ahead. Leading with a long-term vision also encourages other leaders and stakeholders to work more expansively, and promotes a kind of radar-like attunement to the future, constantly questioning today's status quo in relation to tomorrow's possibilities.

Curiosity

Perhaps you've heard the term "beginner's mind." It's a Buddhist expression that describes someone who approaches new situations with openness, willingness, and humility. Too often, traditional leaders will assume that they know or understand something because . . . they're the leaders. Or they'll assume that they don't need to know anything they haven't already mastered. By contrast, curious leaders are always interested in learning and understanding more. If lifelong learning is a prerequisite for surviving in the new economy, the curious leader is an ambitious learner. Curiosity drives someone to understand the intricacies of an important business process, as well as the ability, personality, and character of the people on their team engaged in that process.

Insight

The effective use of insight—the ability to synthesize and distill disparate ideas, events, and issues into an understanding that makes sense to everybody—is vital in a fast-moving and complex economy. Very often, different teams and individuals will be working head-down on a problem or an initiative, but won't really understand (or care to understand) how what they're doing is going to affect the supply chain, the product pipeline, or the whole company. Insight provides the essential perspective. It reminds everyone what they're supposed to be doing and why they're supposed to be doing it. In today's world, the accelerated pace of change, the flattening of hierarchies, and the empowerment of work groups and teams means that leaders have to provide a much greater level of insight. They have to stay ahead of the curve if they're going to continue to give the right guidance in today's more complex environment.

Engagement

Leaders today need to be more in the trenches than ever before. Engagement means that the leader is always up to speed, and always the most committed, most take-charge person on the team. Remember Harry Truman's slogan "the buck stops here"? That sums up the nature of engagement. It captures the need for leaders to show up 100 percent and take complete responsibility for their actions and for the results produced by the entire team.

Determination

Now more than ever, leaders have to be the first ones to arrive in the morning and the last ones to leave at night. Determination is a measure of the leader's energy level, as well as his or her resourcefulness, tenacity, and stamina in the face of challenges, problems, and existential threats.

These six qualities strike me as great aspirational values that spell out ways that you can be successful in what you do, regardless of the position you're looking to attain or the business you want to launch.

GETTING FIRED: TRANSCENDING SHAME

In our society, getting fired has traditionally been a shameful and humiliating experience that people tend to take extremely personally. When we get fired from companies where we've spent a lot of time, made friends, and built our professional identities, we tend to judge ourselves mercilessly. We assume we must have done something terribly wrong thing (or failed to do some imponderable right thing); otherwise, we'd still be there.

People lose jobs for a wide array of reasons, many of which have nothing to do with their abilities, their productivity, or their work ethic—particularly in today's crazy economy. So if you have lost a job, or fear you are about to lose one, the first and most important step is to not take it personally.

I know from painful experience that that's easier said than done. Try to remind yourself that a job loss has very little to do with who you really are or what you are truly capable of doing. The job you lost is one out of a number of life experiences that you can use for your ongoing education and evolution. As much time as you spent there, including the people, the wins, and the losses, it is only a step on the overall path that you are walking. You can ease the feelings of rejection and dislocation by striving for that philosophical "altitude." That perspective is likely something that is far more accessible to you now, at this stage in your life, than it might have been at an earlier time when you weren't quite so seasoned.

This was my experience when I left DreamWorks Animation in 2009. I had been there for six fantastic years, and had helped them grow two departments, one of which I started from scratch. But when the company changed direction late in 2008, the kind of work that I had become known for was on its way out, and I was becoming no longer the right fit for the company.

I remember my defining meeting with the company's COO, one of the most unusual meetings of its kind I had ever had. She said, "We love you, and we love the work you've done, but . . ." She trailed off, trying to find the words. "But I don't know what else there is for you to do here."

She said it with genuine regret, and it was a strange moment for me, having been fired before in more traditional, contentious confrontations. But the reality is that it is tough for companies today to stay competitive without being able to make strategic changes—and it was time for such a change at DreamWorks.

I wasn't surprised to learn that my job was disappearing. I had felt it coming for some months. It was as if I had completed what I had come there to do, and the beautiful flower that had been my job was starting to dry up. I had halfheartedly tried to figure out what else I could do at DreamWorks, but the truth was that I was done there.

In looking back at times when you've lost a job—or in looking at how you're doing in your current job—think about whether you saw or see the signs of an impending separation. Pay attention to the subtle changes that you see around you: the meetings that you stop getting invited to, the cc: lists that you are removed from, the time it takes people to return your calls or answer your emails.

Rather than panicking or trying to disregard these signals, engage with them. Ask questions; figure out why this is happening. It could be an opportunity for you to review and renew your role at the organization, or it could be an indication that you are no longer a good fit. If you can, meet the challenge head on, and use it as a way of making a productive change rather than waiting for a decision to be made for you.

When and if it happens, rather than taking a job loss as a personal failure, see it as a milestone on your journey—a completed experience that you can now add to your portfolio and leverage into another, better opportunity to do what you do best. Accept it, and in the process of accepting it, as I did at DreamWorks, become a partner in the process of your exit—not a victim.

DON'T HIDE YOUR AGE

As I've explained, your résumé is no longer the predominant tool you will use in seeking out new career opportunities. But you will still need a résumé, as well as the online equivalents of your résumé, most importantly your LinkedIn profile. And this raises the question of how you should include your age in your public presence. Should you include real dates that will reveal exactly how old you are, or should you try to obscure them?

One view is that, in order to combat ageism, you should focus strictly on your work so as to avoid distracting a potential employer or client with concerns about your age. You can achieve this by, for example, omitting some of your work positions to appear as if you have a shorter career (and are therefore younger). Many career coaches will tell you to just start your career twenty years ago, and to not list graduation dates for your education.

But I advocate the opposite approach, which is that you should be completely open. Playing defense right out of the box is not a winning strategy. Giving in to prejudice, as any civil rights advocate will tell you, is not the way to combat it. Don't waste your time or their time trying to represent yourself as something you're not. It's like online dating: if you post a younger picture of yourself, your date is going to be annoyed and turned off when you show up to the first meeting. Honesty and integrity matter. If someone is genuinely interested in you only to realize that you've misrepresented yourself on your profile, that doesn't set up a trusting working relationship. If they are ageist, it is highly likely that they will reject you anyway—and fudging your age isn't going to help.

There is a saying, apparently, that goes around in recruiting circles at companies in relation to older job applicants. They talk about whether or not they're willing to consider "hiring Dad" or "hiring Mom" for a position. Face it: we're not going to change attitudes by pretending we're younger and hoping that somehow they won't notice or will like us when they get to know us. And do you really want to work with people who are biased against you from the start? I would hope not. There are more and better opportunities out there for us to both explore and create.

UNEXPECTED BENEFITS OF AGING

Whereas sixty-five used to be the agreed-upon age where most workers were no longer capable of productive contributions in the workplace, today's sixty-five-year-olds are more than likely to look, feel and act as if they are ten years younger. I'm not glibly claiming that "sixty-five is the new fifty-five." Sixty-five is actually the new six- ty-five. It's not the same as fifty-five at all. It's an entirely new experi- ence of life at this age—a radical recalibration of what we're supposed to expect in keeping with the increasing longevity we are witnessing all around us. And if, according to many surveys and studies, most people actually get happier as they age, the longer life we have left will be an increasingly contented one.

Science is discovering a lot of new and positive things about the aging process. We grew up believing that the brain was a fixed entity, a kind of filing cabinet used for storing and retrieving information in a mechanical fashion. According to this concept, once we grew up, we were done—defined by our completed brain. But modern neu- roscience tells us that the mind is increasingly seen as a malleable and changeable part of the body. We are capable of self-motivated, self-evolving core physiological and psychological change all the way through life.

Understanding that the brain and its actual physical capacities can change and grow over time is pretty amazing and definitely en- couraging. Scientists call this neuroplasticity, and it is what enables us to continue to reframe situations, beliefs, and other experiences. It also allows us to evolve our brains into new, more flexible, and more effective engines for living our lives more successfully. So we can change the way we think; we can evolve ourselves into new mind- sets if we want to. This ability underlies the first Boomer Reinven- tion step described in Part III of this book, which is to use Reframing techniques to positively refocus your career direction. We humans are more capable of change than we previously thought.

Neurologists also report that older people tend to have a gift for what they call *gist thinking*—the ability to quickly get to the heart of a subject. You may have experienced this when participating in a meeting or conversation. As others ponder a tough question or problem, you just blurt out the solution—perhaps provoking surprised glances and questions like "How did you know that?" It seems that our years of experience allow us to recognize patterns on an unconscious level. Without really thinking about it, we see through problems because we have had to learn similar solutions many times before.

Additionally, as we get older, we naturally develop a greater capacity for empathy. Perhaps that is due to our own life lessons staring us in the face and causing us to think twice before judging others or their actions. Coupled with gist thinking, this empathic ability makes us ideal candidates for mentoring and problem solving, maybe even elevating us to mystical sage status amongst younger people who come to us for help and support.

YOUR SECOND ACT IS A GIFT: A JUNGIAN VIEW

Here's an encouraging metaphor you can use to reframe the aging period of your life, courtesy of the famous Swiss psychologist Carl Jung.

Imagine that you are standing outside on a sunny day. Think of yourself as a sundial. In the morning, as the sun rises, you cast a long shadow in one direction. As the morning continues, your shadow gets shorter and shorter, until, at noon, you cast no shadow at all, with the sun being directly overhead.

If the shadow is the reference point for our identity, as we get closer to midlife, that reference point becomes shorter and shorter until we completely lose the sense of who we are when the shadow disappears. This parallels the sense of doubt and struggle that we may experience as we plow through life's challenges and uncertainties. The expectations that we may have had as a result of our upbringing or our education get tested and often turn out differently than we expected. Successes may harbor hidden or surprising costs. Failures may trigger deeper, perhaps irrational beliefs and lead to uncontrolled or unexpected behaviors. Relationships may not follow the prescribed path that we were taught, giving rise to conflict and confusion.

In the afternoon of life, something new begins to happen. Just at the moment when we have lost all sense of ourselves, all signposts or points of reference for who we are and what we are actually meant to do with our lives, we begin to cast a shadow again. The key difference is that the shadow is lengthening away from us in a different, opposite direction from the one it took during the morning.

How do we respond to this unexpected change? If we are pining for our cherished former reference point and keep looking for it to reappear, we will be disappointed and perhaps despairing. But if we are willing to turn 180 degrees and take in the whole picture, accepting that there are more possibilities than those that we were taught or became attached to, then we will notice the shadow lengthening in the opposite direction. We can follow it as it extends out into new territory, redefining us in a new way, expanding from zero in a constantly greater, longer, perhaps more profound direction.

By the time the sun sets, and we cease to cast the shadow and merge into the night, we have extended ourselves fully, creating a complete life that reflects our transformation from learner and experimenter into explorer and discoverer.

OK, maybe I'm romanticizing it a bit, but you get the idea: the second half of life is not a process of reduction; it's a process of expansion.

OVERCOMING THE FEAR OF ENTREPRENEURSHIP

The workplace is getting more entrepreneurial—and freelance. It applies to every generation, not just ours. Various surveys estimate that as much as 50 percent of all work will be done on a freelance basis within the next twenty to thirty years. This is becoming known as the "gig economy," and while I can see why some economists fear the collapse of benefits infrastructures and safety nets, this may not be all bad news for boomers who do have at least some measure of support from Medicare and social security.

Many boomers, however, are not thrilled by the idea that, in the years to come, they may need to become more freelance and entrepreneurial in their approach to work. I've gotten into some heated discussions at dinner parties and barbeques talking about this question with other boomers.

They say, "You can't teach entrepreneurship! Entrepreneurs are risk-takers, and not everyone is a risk-taker!" They point to the most well-known entrepreneurs of our time, the ones who have been brilliant, single-minded, charismatic, and, in many cases, lucky. They say that entrepreneurship is a function of personality, and that it is something that is innate.

Sure, there are people who are born entrepreneurs. But entrepreneurship is not all or nothing—there's a spectrum. In times like these, like it or not, we need to at least become *more* entrepreneurial. Wouldn't you rather learn to be more of a master of your destiny versus being passively reliant on someone providing you with a job? Taking managed risks with your career is actually a more secure pathway than simply searching for some job, any job, in your fifties or beyond. If you can begin to accept even a slightly more entrepreneurial path, then you are well on your way to being more successful in today's marketplace.

Each of us has a different set of personality traits and quirks, and some people are more imaginative, extroverted, and risk-tolerant than others. But entrepreneurship is a sandbox where we all can play, to varying degrees and in various roles. If you have been buried in tight hierarchical organizations for the last thirty or more years, you have more choices than to simply seek out yet another insecure, disempowered corporate gig.

As an older person, your circumstances may also be more suited for entrepreneurship than you realize. If you're an empty nester, if you have a spouse or partner who is generating income, if your parents are not a major financial burden to you, if your house is paid off or your mortgage is affordable ... now may be the best time in your life to embrace the calculated risk that is inherent in entrepreneurship.

Furthermore, your life experience gives you a tremendous advantage over younger entrepreneurs. You know so much! You are battle-tested. You are not likely to make the same kinds of mistakes you would have made if you had launched your business thirty years ago. The knocks you've taken and the lessons you've learned will help you avoid pitfalls and chart a smarter way forward.

No wonder research sponsored by the Kauffman Foundation found that older entrepreneurs are twice as likely to be successful in their ventures as younger entrepreneurs.

AND THE STONES ARE STILL TOURING!

If you still have worries about whether a second act is possible for you, think about some of the role models who surround us. It is pretty phenomenal, when you think about it, that one of the top bands of our generation would have continued to tour into their seventies. Back in the 1960s, I don't think any of us would have remotely imagined that the Rolling Stones would stay together for so long—or that Keith would actually be alive half a century a later.

And yet the Rolling Stones aren't the first group of musicians to continue creating well into their golden years. I don't think any of us would have been able to conceive of what an old rock star would look like at seventy. I mean, it was literally something nobody thought about.

When you think about old blues musicians, though, there was never any arbitrary age where blues musicians were supposed to hang up their hats. When we were growing up, the classic blues artists who inspired rock 'n' roll were already getting on in years. They all kept on performing and recording albums into their seventies and eighties. So why would a rocker be expected to hang it up?

Although Neil Young sang, "It's better to burn out than to fade away," and the Who's Pete Townsend declared, "Hope I die before I get old," plenty of the great rock 'n' rollers—including Young and Townsend—have thoroughly reframed those notions, and are still here and still working. If they're still going strong, why shouldn't the rest of us?

What legacy do you want to leave to your family, your friends, and your colleagues? Isn't it time to appreciate yourself for all the work you've done and the lessons you've learned? Isn't it time to translate that into something meaningful, purposeful, and lucrative? Isn't it time to take a chance on yourself?

Part II

PROFILES IN REINVENTION

REINVENTION IS AN EXCITING, NERVE-WRACKING, crazy-making, exhilarating process of inner and outer discovery. Many boomers are already successfully putting it into practice, and I wanted to include a few of their stories to both illustrate the process and provide a bit of inspiration. Changing your career trajectory is, indeed, an attainable goal.

Each of the boomers you'll meet has a unique story. While I was not able to meet or speak with people from every kind of background or experience, these profiles reflect some of the key questions that most people will ponder and deal with in their reinvention, regardless of who they are or what they've done with their lives.

They all started with the need to make some kind of significant shift. None of them just fell into their reinventions. All but one experienced losing one or more jobs as they hit their fifties, and they all decided to take back control of their lives, each in a different way. Planning was not always possible; the outcomes were often surprising. And while a few of them have realized their goals, all of them are still in process in some way, continuing to explore, discover, and further refine their quest, making the practice of reinvention into something of a lifestyle.

I hope you find these stories informative. They'll serve as a real-world reference for the detailed description of the *Boomer Reinvention* methodology that follows in Part III of this book.

Chapter 3.

JOHN PUGLIANO:
THE NEXT CAREER WAS
AWAYS THERE

WHEN THE 2008 RECESSION HIT, John Pugliano realized that he was going to need to figure something out or be swept aside in the turbulence to come. He was in his late forties and knew that if he was laid off, it would be extremely difficult to find a new job. After two decades as a sales executive specializing in industrial and paper products, he knew that he needed to be proactive about his career, but he didn't know what direction to take. The skill set that he had developed for many years as a hobby just didn't seem like a viable career move—until he finally listened to some constructive feedback and reframed some of his ideas.

John did indeed lose his job, and his strong comeback can be traced to his roots as a scrappy blue-collar kid growing up with his brother and their widowed mom in Pennsylvania. He had always been interested in business and became fascinated early on by the stock market and investing. Sitting on the porch of his grandfather's house, he would look over the financial section of the Sunday paper. He had no idea what he was looking at, and no one could really explain it to him, but he knew there was something fascinating about the numbers and the charts and the symbols, and he knew he wanted to learn more about it someday.

When John graduated from high school, he felt he wasn't ready for college and thought it would be a waste of his mother's money, so he enlisted in the Marines. His military service was a win for him: he enjoyed the work and got to see the world, and his experience made him realize the importance of education. He became interested in engineering, science, and thermodynamics. Two years into his four-year enlistment while serving on an aircraft carrier, he had what he calls a "reframing moment" and began to read books for the first time. By the end of his enlistment, he was prepared for college. He was accepted by Penn State as an undergrad and joined the Army ROTC in order to help pay for tuition.

In addition to his basic business classes, John studied environmental science and engineering. That wound up serving him well in his eventual sales career, as it gave him an understanding of the underlying technical characteristics of the products he sold. In his junior year, the Army offered him a Regular Army commission upon graduation. John had an uncle who was a retired career Army officer, so he thought that maybe he could make it work. He was also attracted by the security of a guaranteed job, mindful of the poor economic conditions that continued to plague the rust belt industries of western Pennsylvania. Despite his mother's continued push to get him into a white-collar career and some trepidations about a military career, he signed up for a three-year tour—a decision he wound up regretting.

The Army trained John as a chemical officer because of his degree in environmental science and engineering, but didn't give him the assignment he expected, and he wound up in Germany in 1990 as a low-level second lieutenant in a helicopter battalion. To make the most of his assignment, he took a distance-learning master's degree program offered by USC in information technology and systems management. This brought him to the attention of Mobil Chemical, who recruited him and launched his mainstream corporate career upon the conclusion of his army tour.

He would spend the next twenty years as a sales and marketing executive working with industrial products, starting in plastic film, reactive urethanes, and high-tech substrates, and moving on to industrial paper products, including medical packaging. His work took him all over the country and then the world, including business development projects in Europe, South America, and China.

After working for Mobil and then a smaller company in the industrial chemical field, John found himself itching to take a risk and do something different that would have more upside. He received an offer that he thought would be the gateway to something new, but after six months, it fizzled. He pivoted and wound up as director of sales for a multilevel marketing company in the cosmetics field. To his surprise, he wound up learning a lot. Up to that point, he had always worked on what he calls bigger "tanker" deals (literally, tankers full of chemicals), but working for the cosmetics company was more personal, more about the individual, and more about taking care of the customer. But the rewards were fairly modest, and John remained somewhat dissatisfied with his career.

Around this time, he read a best-selling book called *The Millionaire Next Door* by Dr. Thomas Stanley, which changed the way he looked at money and career. While the book is mostly a business guide to the mindset of wealthy and successful achievers, John was struck by one key idea. As the title suggests, Stanley contends that 80 percent of self-made millionaires are the guys who live next door to you—quiet, low-key, family men who live below the radar. John thought back to when he was a kid, and his neighbors were exactly these guys: the dentist with his practice in his basement, the guy who owned the machine shop, the guy with the small trucking business. These were outwardly unassuming men who wound up leaving significant wealth to their children and the community.

This was a real epiphany for John: he realized he wanted to be that millionaire next door. He wanted to be building a business through creating assets and watching them appreciate, rather than chasing the carrot that was being dangled in front of him in his corporate career. It was 1996, he was thirty-five years old, and he now realized that he just didn't fit into the corporate world. He was something of a contrarian, and he hadn't fit into the bureaucracy of the Army either. In retrospect, he wishes that he had listened more to others who were giving him feedback about his choices—it would have saved him a lot of time along the way to get to where he is today.

One way or another, John knew that he wanted and needed to be an entrepreneur: "Not a Bill Gates entrepreneur, but a hometown entrepreneur." But his wife was pregnant with their fifth child (there would be a sixth down the road), and he knew that he couldn't just come home from work and announce that he was going to leave a secure corporate job—as he had tried unsuccessfully to do with the cosmetics business gig. He had to put his responsibilities first, and he needed the paycheck.

John had been trading stocks since he was a junior in college. The additional income he'd received from his Army ROTC service had allowed him to scrape together a couple thousand dollars and open a Schwab brokerage account, through which he continued to trade off and on. When his epiphany moment happened in 1996, he realized that maybe his interest in the stock market could help him to create the wealth and independence that he admired in the millionaires next door. For John, trading stocks had progressed from a childhood fascination to a hobby, and now he saw the potential for it to become a real source of income: "I was going to take it seriously, I was going to learn how to do it, and I was going to be really good at it."

By the mid-1990s, internet discount brokerages were taking off, and day trading was becoming more common. While John continued to focus on his day job, doing his best to rack up sales, play the game, and earn promotions, his heart wasn't in it. His passion was in cultivating his side gig trading stocks, and hoping it would lead to greater independence.

Before his 1996 epiphany, John had attributed his dissatisfaction with his work to being in the wrong job, so he was always on the lookout for a better gig, thinking that a new job would be a better fit. His realization that he was actually an entrepreneur at heart freed him from the quest for the "perfect job." Ironically, this gave him more energy to focus on the job he had, which meant that he wound up being more productive and thus making more money—which then, of course, supported his stock trading. So for many years, John had a very winning formula.

Eventually a large industrial paper company picked him up. They were looking for someone who combined his scientific and engineering experience with a flair for understanding the consumer. It wasn't a particularly high-profile job, and it was tough to make the transition out of cosmetics and back into industrial sales, but he enjoyed getting back to a steadier salary, better benefits, and higher sales commissions.

It was here that he met his mentor, a man he would work for in this and another job over the next decade. This guy was the best manager John ever had. He cared about business and people. And he supported John because he saw him as an innovator, someone who was willing to experiment and think strategically about where everything was going.

After spending a few years working for another company, he returned to working with his former mentor at a new company that was selling specialty paper filtration products and medical packaging— lines that John was very familiar with. The job expanded beyond sales into new product development, including a carbon fiber paper project that John was very enthusiastic about. He loved the product work, even if he didn't like the way the company was being managed.

But what kept him engaged and made the corporate career viable was that he cared about the people he worked with, and especially about his customers. As a matter of integrity and a point of pride, he wanted to make sure that he and his products could deliver on their promises. For John, "the best job security is taking care of your customers." And with his boss's protection, he was pretty much left to do his job. But he also knew that eventually, his penchant for challenging the status quo could sabotage his career. If profitable product line sales drastically declined, funding for his innovative development projects would be the first programs cut.

John was finding it more and more uncomfortable going to work. He saw the existential business threats that nobody wanted to talk about or deal with. Big paper companies were consolidating in the face of these economic factors, particularly due to digital technology. It was particularly frustrating to witness upper management's entrenched mentality that didn't want to see the handwriting on the wall. He would sit silently in staff meetings, knowing his colleagues wouldn't like his controversial ideas.

John knew that he would have to change his direction soon, and he continued to trade stocks to build his nest egg. That was where his passion was, but it never occurred to him that he could turn that passion into an actual business. He wasn't very taken with the financial sector ("I thought it was a 'dirty' industry") and he hadn't cultivated any contacts despite being very involved in trading.

By 2009, John's net worth had grown from about $70k when he began trading seriously in 1996 to over $1 million. With six kids, he wasn't ready to retire by any stretch, but he had built up a certain amount of leverage that he hoped would let him make more strategic decisions about his career. He decided it was time to start pushing back on his corporate career limitations and to start figuring out a sustainable career plan.

He thought about opening a small industrial, manufacturing, or franchise business in Atlanta, where he was living, but as time went on, and he continued to chafe under the difficult working environment at the home office, he persuaded the company to let him move to Salt Lake City, where he could continue to oversee his accounts and his other assignments, and spend less time distracted by the politics at company headquarters.

In the midst of his family's move west, John and his brother also had to deal with their mother's declining health. They had to move her out of her house in Pennsylvania, first to Florida to live briefly with his brother, and then to John's new home in Salt Lake City, where she would, sadly, continue to decline before passing away less than two years later, on John's fifty-first birthday.

John hung on to his job, remaining in a quandary about how to transition to a millionaire-next-door venture, until he learned that it was possible to get registered as an investment advisor without having to be affiliated or employed by a registered broker/dealer. He had never known anyone who had started a financial advisory from scratch; he had always thought that he needed sponsorship from a big firm. More important, he discovered that with an advisor's license, he could use discrete trading authority to directly manage a client's portfolio. This meant that he would not be limited to simply offering advice or preparing financial plans. He could actually trade for his clients using the same strategies that he had used to build his own wealth.

But who would trust him? He just didn't think that anyone would actually hire him to advise them on stock purchases, much less handle their portfolios. But his wife encouraged him, saying, "People ask you for stock advice all the time!" He realized that she was right: he had advised family members, and one coworker had even signed a power of attorney so that John could manage her IRA portfolio.

Meanwhile, conditions continued to deteriorate at work, and then his beloved carbon fiber project was canceled, so John decided to give entrepreneurship a shot. He spent the rest of 2012 planning how he was going to pivot in this new direction. In the end, he took the Series 65 exam to be licensed as an investment advisor and then set up a limited liability corporation (LLC). By March 2013, he was licensed in the state of Utah and was ready to begin his first entrepreneurial endeavor, while remaining on the job at the paper company.

Guided by the Stephen Covey maxim "Begin with the end in mind," John visualized himself at age sixty-five, continuing to work and enjoying his successful advisory practice. He was going to focus on clients in their forties to their sixties, who still had earning years ahead, who would be comfortable with a certain level of risk, and who would not necessarily need a recurring income stream from their portfolios. He would invest their money the same way that he invested his own, and in the process he hoped to create real wealth for his clients.

That same month, John's boss and mentor at the paper company quit in frustration. He, too, had been unhappy with the direction that the company was taking. John thought about quitting in solidarity with his boss, but realized the smarter course of action was to ride it out and let them fire him. After all, he had his new license, but he had no clients and no business yet.

The next six months at work were chaotic and nearly intolerable. John was swamped with assignments that were not part of his job description, endless reporting, and intense scrutiny over minute details. Clearly, they were trying to get him to quit. If John had been a lifetime corporate exec in his mid-fifties, he imagines it would have been horrific—waking up and going to work every day with the fear that he was going to get fired. But John had teed up his new career, so he had something to work toward in the midst of increasing pressure and toxicity in his job.

Every day, the light at the end of the tunnel was getting brighter. Freedom was within reach.

The expected phone call came toward the end of September: his new boss was going to be in Salt Lake and wanted to meet at the airport.

John knew the drill. When he showed up at the airport hotel conference room, his boss was there, along with the senior vice president of human resources. They had both flown all the way from Atlanta just to fire him. It was all over in a few minutes. They handed him the paperwork to sign, and it was done.

They characterized his firing as a "re-org." John was being laid off along with a twenty-five-year-old woman in another department. Of course, firing two people in a company of over two thousand could hardly be classified as an organizational change. This was their way of protecting themselves against any accusations of job discrimination—either from John accusing them of age discrimination, or from the young woman accusing them of sex discrimination. It was a well-orchestrated corporate move, down to the cover provided by the HR exec—his presence making sure that there was a third party witness to the meeting, and a trained professional to mediate any unexpected unpleasantness. John laughs about the paranoia motivating these execs: "They could have done it over the phone—it wouldn't have mattered to me."

Fortunately, John was already well along the path to his reinvented career. But even so, he still felt vulnerable. John had no idea whether or not his new venture would actually work. His Plan B would be to stay in the industrial paper business. And because John had done a good job of taking care of and staying in touch with his suppliers, customers, and competitors over the years, he did indeed get some calls when the word got out that he had been fired. But when he talked to one company, he realized he would have to jump through the same corporate hoops—which he had no intention of doing.

So John started networking in earnest, beginning with the friend whose IRA portfolio he had been trading under the power of attorney. She became one of his first clients. He also decided to launch a regular blog as a way of sharing his views and attracting business. His approach was to write only about things that he felt were important and of interest.

This was, in retrospect, a crucial decision. He didn't sign up an enormous number of people to the blog, but the ones who did sign up were the people who appreciated his point of view.

He conceived of his business as a face-to-face concierge-style practice where he would go around and meet people and get them to sign up to his service. His model was Warren Buffett, who in his early days famously went around Omaha and signed up a group of doctors who were willing to invest with him. So John started going around to find people who were millionaire-next-door types—the people he admired for their values and their attitude.

This is where John's authenticity came into play, and where he had a strong advantage. He knew that his most likely prospects were people with a philosophy about money that resembled his: "I'm not the guy in the fancy suit with the Rolex watch. I've still got my western Pennsylvania accent. I'm still driving a thirteen-year-old minivan." Knowing and accepting who he was became one of the keys to his successful reinvention. Perhaps for the first time in his career, he was able to be completely himself, completely transparent, and completely enthusiastic about what he was doing. That is a powerful proposition for someone starting a new business, and a powerful and convincing pitch to a prospective client.

In the two years that John has been running his financial advisory business, he has never gone to a Chamber of Commerce event or done any of the others things that experts will tell you to do to launch your business. He still doesn't know anyone else in the financial services industry. He is just following his own ideas, doing his own research, and investing as smartly as he can. The people he does know are his clients—mostly small-business owners, corporate IT people, and medical professionals. He has gone from that one friend with her IRA to over forty clients and more than $16 million under management.

John initially thought the business would spread entirely by word of mouth. However, he soon realized that the blog was also starting to bring in clients. He then started podcasting—almost by accident. Over the Fourth of July weekend in 2014, he read some investment advice by a famous financial pundit that really ticked him off. Try as he might, he couldn't find anyone presenting a meaningful counterargument, so he recorded a critique as a podcast and posted it. He had been interviewed once on a friend's podcast, and had been a ham radio operator way back when, so he understood the technical process. But mostly, he realized that he just had something to say—and that the digital world was a place where he could say it.

That first podcast led to another ten episodes, and he is now approaching two hundred episodes in his series. It has been an eye-opening experience. John has developed a great relationship with his audience and gets regular feedback. The podcasts now constitute an archive of John's opinions and predictions about the market. Anyone who might be thinking of hiring John to manage their portfolio only has to pull up that archive and listen to what he had to say a year ago or six months ago, and they'll understand who he is, how he invests his money, and whether his approach is right for them.

John's podcasts are very basic in style: "I don't have a broadcast voice, I mispronounce words and talk in incomplete sentences, I don't have a catchy slogan or a theme song, and I haven't written a best-selling book. I just say what I believe to be true." But on the day of our conversation, he looked up his ranking, and the podcast was in thirteenth place on the iTunes store under the Investing category. He has about ten thousand regular listeners.

It's a long story with a happy ending. John loves his clients. His clients love him. He makes himself accessible to them pretty much 24–7 because the financial world is constantly changing—and he loves that challenge. His main takeaway is that you don't have to squeeze yourself into some kind of box to have a career: "I've got at least ten years until I'm sixty-five. These are going to be the peak earning years of my life. I'm going to be earning a really nice income doing exactly what I want to do."

Chapter 4

JUDY CONTRERAS:
TRUST YOUR INSTINCTS, DO YOUR HOMEWORK

IN 2014, AFTER BEING FIRED FROM three corporate HR jobs in a row, Judy Contreras asked herself this question: "Am I going back to corporate, or am I going to steer my own ship?"

Since then, this scrappy mother of three has bravely turned her life around, forsaking the uncertainties of corporate life for a chance to build a long-term career where she is in control.

Judy's corporate experience reads like a primer of the worst practices in corporate America. Judy experienced too many layoffs and too much time between jobs. At a certain point, she decided that she didn't want to be always on the waiting end of the career equation, ultimately being stuck with an inadequate severance package.

After a divorce in 1998, Judy resurrected the HR career that she had put on the back burner to raise her daughters. She spent the next fifteen years working hard to take care of her kids. The word "loser" was not part of her vocabulary.

Flash forward to 2013. Judy was laid off from her job as a corporate HR manager. She decided to go out on her own and reinvent her career. Judy spent the better part of a year laying the groundwork for her second act, doing the necessary research, and getting coaching and mentoring to iron out the uncertainties and fill in the unknowns. She is now a couple of years into building a sales practice as a consultant/

broker for franchise business. She acquires leads and sets them up with the appropriate franchise business that meets their needs and aspirations. As she says in the audio promo on her LinkedIn profile, she's "helping you build your own dreams before someone else hires you to build theirs."

Judy has always been ambitious. Her parents were immigrants and wanted her to get on a doctor/lawyer track. She graduated from high school on a Friday, and the following Monday she started college—which she completed in three years. When she graduated from college on a Friday, the following Monday she started grad school to earn an MBA. And then she crashed.

She was just twenty-two years old when she came out of grad school. Her parents were disappointed she hadn't gone to law school. But the way she looked at it, her friends who went to law school all had connections that got them entry-level law jobs. Judy's parents owned a grocery store. How was she supposed to get a job as a lawyer?

She wound up in financial services, collecting and lending money. The financial services firm where she worked operated on a commission-plus-bonus model, and she thrived. She learned from the start that she had a knack for follow-up and converting prospects to buyers. In some ways, her job was great. It paid well and offered good benefits: "I made some good money, I bought my first car. I bought my first house."

But Judy also had doubts about the ethical basis of the business she was in. The company was a lender to Ford Motor Co., and Judy got to see how the money they were lending was being used. In one deal, Ford borrowed $65 million to buy industrial robots, which resulted in large layoffs of assembly-line workers who'd been doing repetitive tasks. Judy was bothered by this: "What's going to happen to these people?" she wondered.

She felt uncomfortable being a part of something that was displacing workers and ruining their lives. So she decided to quit her job and do something that would allow her to help people, look after them, and take care of them. This switch led her first into office management and then into human resources (HR).

She found a job as **an** office manager in a small company, where she was also tasked with handling HR. She had no idea how to do HR, so she decided to go back to school to get a special credential as a Senior Professional Human Resources (SPHR) manager. Over the course of twenty years with a succession of companies, she rose from office manager to HR director to vice president. The first years were great—hiring and filling job openings, granting raises and promotions, conducting trainings, and administering benefits. She felt good about handling human capital. As better opportunities came her way, she seized them, building a very solid reputation and deep experience in the HR world, not only in the direct management of staff but in strategic analysis of HR best practices. Judy dealt with occupational safety (OSHA) issues, labor negotiations, enterprise software installations, leadership development, legal issues, and more.

Most of her employers were straight-shooters, but she did run into the occasional bad actor. This got worse during and following the 2008 recession. The company she was working for at the time wasn't doing well. She realized that they were going to need to lay off employees because both demand and income had fallen precipitously. Within months, she was forced to help the owners shut down the entire company.

Judy sees the recession as causing a sea change in HR practices and management behavior toward employees. Raises and promotions are few and far between, staff development has been reduced, benefits are being cut, and employees are being asked to take on a greater percentage of the costs. These changes left Judy feeling much less positive about her career.

Judy found herself fired from a company when she refused to hire illegal immigrants to fill 1,800 openings that could have gone to U.S. citizens. She went to a healthcare company for about a year and witnessed the new CEO perform a wholesale layoff of long-term staffers (ostensibly to hire new employees at cheaper rates). She worked for a retailer for about six months that she felt was behaving unethically toward their employees. The company had major turnover issues (70 percent) and had not given raises in five years. The final straw was a move that management made under the guise of adjusting their health benefits plan to conform to the Affordable Care Act. They had Judy jack up the medical deductible to a very high rate, and they then used the money that they saved to finance a new retail location. When Judy protested, they let her go.

Corporate work was clearly becoming a dead end. Judy figured it would take her another year to find the next job, which would only lead to another layoff. She felt that it was time to break that cycle. She was prepared to take a risk, so long as it wasn't something reckless. Once she made the decision to go forward, she disconnected from the job search engines and stopped all the automated reminders and other distractions.

She looked at taking her savings and buying into a franchise business, but couldn't find one that made sense to her. She began asking the franchise broker she was working with about what he did, thinking that his work and lifestyle made more sense for her personality. He was a little reluctant to talk to her about becoming a broker—it would, after all, be competitive with what he was doing, and it wouldn't earn him a commission. She laughs: "He would have rather sold me a Supercuts!" The more Judy learned about being a franchise broker, the more she liked the idea. But she was a bit nervous about getting into an entirely new business. She toyed with the idea of staying in HR in a consulting capacity.

Judy felt she needed an outside perspective before she pulled the trigger on any decision. So she sought help from the Small Business Administration (SBA), which offers business coaching for prospective small business owners. It's a free service that she highly recommends. Local SBA offices maintain lists and relationships with coaches and mentors who will work with you to evaluate your needs and help you find the right person to work with you. Judy was methodical about finding the right coach. She didn't want to go by the résumé alone, and so she talked to a number of candidates on the phone and visited with them in person. It took her five weeks to finally find someone who understood her and whose advice she felt she could believe and respect.

Working with her SBA coach, she compared and contrasted the possible business scenarios, and her coach played devil's advocate, trying to get to the bottom of what she was most interested in and what level of risk she was comfortable with. She was concerned that she wouldn't be successful as an HR consultant both because of the way the whole business was trending, and also because there were much bigger players who would be hard to compete with.

In the end, the scale tipped toward the franchise consultant/broker business. In weighing the pros and cons, she felt that it was better to put her money into franchise consulting because it was a turnkey operation. She would be provided with all the tools and training she needed to launch it. She presented the coach with a cash-flow projection for the first year of the consulting business. He cut her projection in half, on the theory that it would be better to plan for a worst-case scenario. In that first year, she had projected that she would close four franchise sales. She actually closed three— so in retrospect, she was grateful to her coach for setting more realistic expectations.

To get started as a franchise consultant/broker, she paid an opportunity fee to a consolidator who markets for franchisors. In exchange, she received training, resources, and access to hundreds of franchisors looking to sign up prospective business owners. This arrangement allowed her to hang out her own shingle (www.ownyournextcareer.com), brand herself, and keep 100 percent of her broker commissions from the franchisor. The practice reminded her a lot of recruiting employees, which enhanced her comfort level.

The whole process reflected Judy's personality. She needed to carefully spend time evaluating her new business, taking the time to get the information she needed to make the decision. "It's still scary," she says. "It's still risky in the sense that you have to make that leap of faith that it's going to work." But the research she did gave her a certain degree of comfort before taking her leap.

It was a big leap. She was coming from the apparent comfort of a W2 job: "That's what I had to get over. I'm not twenty years old anymore." She had to get over the loss of that regular paycheck and the benefits—and the 401(k) plan. She knew it was a big risk, and she was giving up a lot. But she had been so frustrated, and was so fed up with her corporate experience, that it seemed like it was worth the try.

Knowing that she needed to buy herself as much time as possible to give the business a chance to get established, Judy lowered her overhead. She owned her house free and clear, so all she needed to do was trim everything except basic living expenses, utilities, and taxes. She simplified her lifestyle, taking advantage of a food bank and the state medical system.

Today her work routine is a demanding one. She starts her day at 7:00 a.m., a good time to start talking with prospects on the east coast from her home in Chicago, and she works until 4:30 or 5:00 p.m. She has become a good time manager, but it didn't start out that way. Initially, in learning mode, she was probably putting in eighty hours per week, which started to take a toll on her. So she incorporated some discipline and shortcuts into the process and now keeps her commitment to a fifty-hour week.

But Judy doesn't screw around. She is constantly mining for prospects. She initially tried purchasing leads from a supplier who captures forms from people interested in buying a franchise business. It was expensive, anywhere from $25 to $150 per lead, and she spent $4,000 on leads without producing a single sale. Now she uses more organic methods: she goes to seminars and outplacement centers, looking for displaced workers. She'll offer to place one of her brochures in a layoff or exit package, which is a win-win for the worker and the former employer. She has built a large referral network on LinkedIn and posts regularly on the platform, as well as contacting prospects directly. In many cases, she looks for people who are quietly looking to get out of their current jobs or who are thinking about a business they can own after retirement. She has also rekindled her relationships from her HR years, which is a great resource—particularly when she hears that a big company is going through layoffs. Many of those individuals could be interested in investing their severance or exit package proceeds into a new business. Her HR background also seems to lend her credibility in her new identity.

When prospecting, Judy typically makes fifty to a hundred contacts per day. When she found that she wasn't getting as much yield as she liked from phone calls, she tried texting and found it produced a much higher (14 percent) response rate. She keeps experimenting with different tweaks, evaluating how each prospect responds, changing the questions she asks, and constantly modifying her pitch. She continues to research methodology and work on her own perceptual skills, training herself to listen for and identify certain common catchphrases and intonations that people use so that she can better address their concerns and land a sale. It winds up saving her time and effort.

It's an iterative process, trying to find the sweet spot. At times, she finds herself feeling jealous of other consultants in her circle who are making more deals. She talked to another broker who sold ten franchises last year—but he had to invest $60,000 to land those deals. By contrast, in Judy's first seven months in business, she closed three deals and spent $4,000. By my calculation, her friend is spending $6k per deal, while Judy is only spending $1,300. She's still trying to figure out how to gain more leverage. Her goal is to return five or six times her investment on each deal she closes.

Some of Judy's friends and family members think she's nuts: "They like the comfort of a job—the security blanket." She tries to explain to them that this is a long-term project. Her goal is to have a business she can do well into retirement, either full- or part-time, providing ongoing income, mental stimulation, and the satisfaction of helping people to become independent and secure in their own businesses.

Judy goes through periods of doubt, of course, where she wonders whether she made the right career decision. But she also knows that playing the "coulda, woulda, shoulda" game is pointless. She is grateful for what she's learned and for the challenges she has overcome. "Now that I've been working to sell businesses, I have a lot more brain power and education and insight into how to do it." She is especially glad that she no longer has to deal with the problems and issues that she was working on in her HR career, where everything she did was for someone else's benefit.

In some ways, Judy is still operating along the same principles that propelled her into HR: the urge to help people to be their best and to be valued and recognized. One of the reasons Judy is so committed to this line of work is that it fulfills her long-standing aspiration to be the master of her own destiny. Still, her mom keeps rubbing her struggles in her face: "If you had gone to law school, you would have had your own business well before now. . . ."

Like Judy, many boomers have friends or family who, out of their concern for us, are grasping for explanations for why we find ourselves needing to reinvent our careers in our fifties or sixties. They mean well, but their attempts to advise us or second-guess our choices are usually irrelevant and rarely helpful. The truth is that Judy might not have been more successful or more prepared for today if she had gone to law school and stuck to that profession. And Judy gets that—after all, she says, "I wound up here and having my own business anyway!"

The truth is that we all wind up with the careers we have because of who we are, not because of what we do—which is one good reason not to waste time or energy beating yourself up over decisions you made in the past. Instead, like Judy, focus on making today and tomorrow the best they can be.

Chapter 5.

DAVID BEADLE:
IF THE VISION IS RIGHT, THE OBSTACLES DON'T MATTER

WHEN DAVID BEADLE WAS SERVED with the lawsuit that would redefine his life, he was on the way out the door to his second wedding. His fiancée was pregnant with his first child, and suddenly he learned that he was being sued for $2 million. "My identity, my company, my ego, just blew up," he recalls.

As an environmental systems engineer, David had founded and built a waste management company in Bakersfield, CA, that serviced the oil and gas industry, a prime driver of the Central Valley economy. David was driven to achieve more and never felt quite satisfied with his progress as a businessman. So when clients approached him about taking on new work, he began expanding his focus to include environmental safety issues as well as hazardous waste removal and remediating mold contamination. In retrospect, he took on work that he shouldn't have, leaving him open to the lawsuit that would ultimately drive him out of his business and into his reinvention.

As David was putting increasing pressure on his business, his personal life was also under stress. After a first marriage failed, David was eager to get married again and to start a family. He found himself drinking too much to cope with it all. Seeking a way to better understand himself and exercise more control over his behavior, he began going to twelve-step meetings. But twelve-step wasn't for him. He didn't feel supported by the process and felt he had to find a way to "let myself accept my own truth"—to find the courage to go with his gut feelings and to overcome the feelings of unworthiness that had long plagued him.

Raised in a very conservative Midwestern evangelical family, David found that his upbringing was holding him back. He realized that he needed to get to the point where he could give himself permission to have a relationship with God on his own terms rather than living by a set of criteria that he felt had been imposed on him from some outside source. He needed to reframe how he saw himself in the world and get to a place where he could accept himself as good enough, flaws and all.

A friend at one of the twelve-step meetings suggested that he look into meditation and recommended an upcoming silent Vipassana yoga retreat in Yosemite. David was intrigued. He had always appreciated the sense of peace he felt in quiet places, so the idea of spending ten days away in nature was attractive, even though the idea of sitting in silence for ten days sounded totally intimidating.

Showing up in Yosemite was a huge leap of faith for David. He didn't know exactly what the ten days was going to be about. He didn't know any of the other participants. It was a completely new experience and was way out of his comfort zone. But he showed up just the same, convinced that there could be something here that was of value, and that he really had nothing to lose. So he just decided to surrender to whatever was going to happen and see how he felt about it.

The first meditation included a little bit of explanation and conversation, but for the next nine days, there would be no talking. Initially, the regimentation and sense of isolation reminded David of a much earlier time in his life when he'd had the misfortune to spend a couple of nights in jail: he was going to have to wake up every morning at 4:30 a.m. and meditate until 9:00 p.m. with only a few breaks. He had been taught to be terrified of just being quiet, because according to his upbringing, that was when the "bad forces" were supposed to come in. But David knew he needed a new approach to his life, so he persisted, and the retreat wound up becoming an incredible, life-changing experience for him.

The first few days of the retreat were a gradual quieting and clearing of the mind. David was proud of the fact that he was able to sit there and just breathe. He felt as if he was watching a documentary of his life unspooling in front of him. His senses became very acute, and he became very aware of his breathing and of the sensations around and inside of his body. He felt as if what he calls "cartoon energy" was flowing out of the top of his head. And then this question appeared: "What do I want to do?" He thought about his capabilities, and about what he enjoyed doing, and specifically about the joy he experienced in sharing his knowledge with others.

On the sixth day, seemingly out of nowhere, he came up with an idea for a new and different business that resonated instantly and deeply with him—something that would get him out of the environmental field, but would still leverage the expertise that he had accumulated through his years in business. He saw what it would look like and how he would go about setting it up. He thought about it for the entire sixth day of the retreat, through multiple meditation sessions, envisioning how it would integrate with the other aspects of his life that he wanted to incorporate.

The vision started tailing off by the end of the day, but David felt profoundly changed. He felt like Moses coming off the mountain. He had a purpose! It was an electric feeling, and he realized that this retreat had been an absolute necessity.

When he returned to Bakersfield, he got to work. The idea for the business was to create a global document-sharing resource for industrial and technical professionals—an e-commerce site for engineers and other subject-matter experts to post and sell technical documents. His environmental business was still on the front burner, and he continued to manage his various accounts and supervise the seven field technicians on his staff. But he started to lay the groundwork for the online business, doing research, gathering documentation he needed, seeking out people to advise him, and building up a functioning network.

In retrospect, David feels that he wasn't very good at vetting his thought process. He was operating perhaps too much on a gut level and not checking out the feedback and the referrals he was getting. He wound up limiting his network to people he met locally, which ended up being a mistake as the online software community in the Bakersfield area was not particularly deep. Nevertheless, he met a developer who he hired to develop the website for him, and within nine months of his return from the retreat, it was up and running.

In the midst of all this, David and his girlfriend decided to get married. It appeared as though most of what David had been dreaming of was about to come true.

But soon after the launch, on the day of David's wedding, the lawsuit hit. It was triggered by a dissatisfied customer on a mold removal project. David had all the lab tests. Everything was aboveboard. But the plaintiff proceeded anyway. The effects were immediate. David's Errors and Omissions insurance premiums went from $3,800 per year to $45,000 per year with a $10,000 deductible. He knew that he couldn't run his business under those conditions. He tried to hang on, and took a second mortgage on his house to support the added costs of running the business. At its peak, he had been booking over $1 million in sales per year, but after a year of struggling, he filed bankruptcy on the business. The financial impact also meant he had to shut down his fledgling website operation.

Concerned about his employees, he called his main competitor, an engineer who also serviced oil and gas industry clients, and asked him to hire his guys and to go after his contracts. The engineer agreed to help, bought David's equipment and inventory, and hired his techs. If David couldn't save his business, at least the people who depended on him wouldn't have to suffer.

Because of new bankruptcy laws, he was facing the need to go through "means testing," meaning that 50 percent of his earnings would go to his creditors for a period of five years. It was not a great option. He had not earned any money for the prior three months, and had technically been unemployed for the past two months. His lawyer, however, was able to negotiate a better outcome and he was able to avoid the five-year obligation, which he hoped would give him the chance to start anew.

Just before the Christmas holidays in 2010, the lawsuit was dismissed. A condition of the dismissal was that David wouldn't be able to countersue, but he was relieved that the whole episode was over and that his reputation had been exonerated.

But despite this good news, he was not able to put the rest of his life back together. Less than four months later, due in part to having to refinance his house to shore up his business, he would have to file personal bankruptcy as well. As he says, "My entire formula for making a living had been taken away from me."

Now he needed a job, a concept that he thought he would never have to contemplate after being self-employed for almost two decades. He pounded the pavement and wound up in a short-term position working for the State of California, but then was dealt another blow. The day after his birthday, his wife booted him out of the house and filed for divorce.

If the bankruptcy crushed his ego, the divorce tore his heart apart. This was undoubtedly the lowest moment of his entire life. His first divorce had been akin to a business split—just a division of assets. This divorce was so painful because he was now a parent, and in the contentiousness with his wife, he was afraid that he would never see his daughter again.

One hopeful development helped keep his finances and his spirit intact. Through his membership in a professional association, he noticed an online job posting at California State University's Bakersfield campus for a safety director. The position required certifications David had, although they were also looking for someone with a risk management background, which he didn't have. But they hired him anyway. The salary was less than what he had been making at his own company, but at least there would be health benefits. It was a nine-to-five job, very procedural, all about forms and meetings, but it saved him.

About four months later, another piece of good fortune landed in his lap. The competitor who had taken over his employees and his accounts called him up and asked to hire him. David wound up consulting for him while still holding onto the university gig. This was a good thing, too, because he found that his credit rating had plummeted. Even though he was paying his wife 50 percent of his earnings as alimony for a period of three years, she had stopped making house payments. So he had to settle for a short sale on his house to square everything away.

Between the university gig and the consulting, David was making enough for the alimony and a modest living. But he felt that he had to leave Bakersfield. The weight of all of the disruptions was just too much, and he needed to start a new life without driving down the same streets and seeing the same people.

He made some inquiries and found that a position similar to the one he had was opening up at the Cal State Long Beach campus. The major drawback would be the two-and-a-half-hour drive each way to see his daughter for visitations.

The Long Beach gig paid a little bit better, but between the costs of the move and waiting for his first paycheck, he wound up living like a monk for the first month—catching fish out of the Pacific Ocean surf break and boiling rice from a fifty-pound bag. This surreal existence was not quite what he had expected in his late forties. Rather than bemoan his life as "horrible," he chose to say that he had wiped the slate clean. All he really needed was to be able to see his daughter. Everything else could wait.

He felt that he wanted to start dating again. He needed the company and the sense of possibilities and connections that come along with exploring relationships. Through eHarmony, he met a woman who would become a friend and who took him under her philosophical wing. She would turn him on to a graduate-level spiritual psychology program that gave him a forum and a process to reset his personal and professional goals. Best of all, the program was structured to cater to working professionals and included a personal project mentoring process. He seized on this feature as a means to workshop and re-launch his online document-sharing business.

Coincidentally, the State of California had passed legislation increasing environmental safeguards in oil and gas production, so David's experience and certifications suddenly became more marketable. He quickly found himself inundated with work. He would consult with all industry clients before he went to work at the university and then late into the evening after he got home, working the equivalent of two full-time jobs. Additionally, he was spending one weekend per month attending and studying in the psychology program.

David was working harder than he had ever worked in his life. He had everything at stake, but he never felt panicked or overwhelmed—just determined. He was learning to be okay with all of it. He understood that he had to give up his preconceptions about what his life should be. When he did that, it all started coming together.

And in the midst of all of this activity, he fell in love. It happened over the course of many months, and in perfect harmony with everything else that was going on with him. For the first time, he was experiencing what it was like to find peace and understanding in a relationship.

David marveled at how the money had come to him when he really needed it—and enough to cover exactly what he needed it to cover: school, his apartment, alimony, child-support, and, of course, the development money for the relaunch of his business.

This time, he did it right—creating a prototype "wire-frame" of the website, investing in trademarks and other intellectual property to brand the site and launch it properly. He even conducted an Indiegogo campaign to raise some extra cash and further market his business through social media. At fifty-six years old, he realized he had to jump into this new medium, writing a blog and interacting with people. "It's amazing how many people I can touch for free!" he recalls.

Interestingly, after the major cash crunch needed to get the business up and running, his consulting income began to tail off. It was as if the universe had rallied to get him all set up, and then when he was ready to launch, it stepped back to let David take over. His income had risen in proportion to his intention and his real need.

Envisioning the outcome, seeing where he wanted to go, was important. His experience clarified that process for him: "If you see it, and start taking steps, you'll always get there in some form. It comes the way it's intended to be. It may not look exactly the way you thought it would be." He realized that he had to give up the rigidity in his thinking.

After seven years with Cal State University, David was able to retire and receive medical benefits. His consulting business brought him back to Bakersfield for a spell, but he and his new girlfriend eventually got married, and he moved back to the Los Angeles area where he now continues to consult and run his new business.

David's business builds off a key digital-era paradigm—that sharing information is a more powerful model than hoarding information. In the analog age, scarcity was the driving force in the marketplace. But in a digital world, where everything has become commoditized, more information and more data are needed to keep up with the pace of change. David's business leverages this need for information. David recognizes that the concept that technical information can be localized and packaged is still hard for many to accept: "For a lot of us, there is a fear of sharing." At the end of the day, however, accumulated knowledge is valuable, and that idea will hopefully keep David in business for the foreseeable future.

Looking back on his reinvention, David is now able to "laugh about this. . . . The whole episode with the bankruptcy, the divorce, all hitting at the same time. I wanted to reinvent myself in some way. What challenges us to do that, other than these episodes? I finally had to do it. In my twenties, I thought knew everything. In my thirties, I was questioning. In my forties, it was fifty-fifty. In my fifties, I don't know shit! So [what's important?]: the spiritual, emotional relationships. . . ."

He and his wife live in a modest apartment and are looking to buy a home. His daughter and her mom moved to New Mexico, and he's okay with that move; he's going to make it work out. He'll find consulting work there so he can spend time near his daughter—maybe open up a new region for one of his clients.

The way he sees things, his life is now a huge adventure. "I keep rolling with the changes. The more things there are to do, the more I like it. . . . I have an incredible partner. My daughter is healthy and smart. What more could I ask for?"

Chapter 6.

MARILYN FRIEDMAN: FINDING RENEWAL IN SURPRISING PLACES

MARILYN FRIEDMAN LOST HER JOB as head of DreamWorks Animation's university outreach program after almost twenty years at the company (and its predecessor, computer graphics studio Pacific Data Images). A talent development and recruiting executive, Marilyn had successfully survived many of the ups and downs at this innovative company, and despite being a self-styled contrarian who liked to buck the system, she had worked like hell, was loyal, and had achieved great success with her programs.

In 2012, DreamWorks was going through tough times, and Marilyn knew the layoffs were coming. As a senior executive, she had been briefed on the company's plans, but she believed she was in the clear, having cut 25 percent of her department's budget.

When the head of HR walked into her office that morning, she thought he was there to discuss the layoff announcements that were being made later that day. Not until he shut the door quietly and regretfully began, "So, you know, the company has had to make some tough decisions lately . . ." did Marilyn realize what was happening. She, too, was being let go.

Marilyn and I were colleagues at DreamWorks, and I wanted very much to include her story in the book. She grew up in New Haven, CT, the daughter of Holocaust survivors. Their ordeal was a difficult legacy, but it gave her a sense of perspective that helps her deal with moments of adversity, even if the situation itself is very traumatic.

Like many teenagers in our generation, and particularly in light of her parents' background, Marilyn signed up for an independent study program to study overseas to "find herself." She wound up spending about six months on an Israeli kibbutz, and even if she didn't quite find herself, she found the man she would eventually marry, Basil Friedman. She then traveled through Europe before coming back to the U.S., reuniting with and then marrying Basil and completing her sociology degree at the University of Colorado.

Basil had earned a business/accounting degree but hated the idea of becoming an accountant. What he really wanted to do was become a chef, so the young couple moved to the San Francisco Bay Area, where Basil enrolled in the California Culinary Academy.

Marilyn had no specific career ambition. Her plan: get the most interesting job out of the want ads (remember the want ads?). She wound up becoming office manager for a creative services agency engaged in designing and printing corporate communications, annual reports, product brochures, and seminar materials. The job introduced her to the very vibrant San Francisco creative community and led to her becoming the studio manager for a preeminent San Francisco graphic designer, who was looking for someone to help him run and grow his studio.

Marilyn loved her job, but after a few years she quit to look for another challenge. At the same time, Basil had begun what would become a successful career in advertising and publishing as a food stylist, working with photographers and commercial production houses.

Marilyn received a couple of offers but wasn't very interested in the jobs she was seeing until she learned of an opening at Pacific Data Images (PDI), a young computer graphics company in Sunnyvale. PDI gave tours of their facility every Friday, so she signed on for a tour, was impressed—and left her résumé.

At this time, the company had about sixty employees, and the interview process ultimately entailed meeting most of them. Clearly, this was a very tight-knit and collaborative culture where everyone had to be the right fit.

Marilyn was hired into a new position as a talent recruiter, splitting off the "people" aspect of production from the scheduling and technical sides. Tech companies were taking off, and computer-generated (CG) visual effects were in demand. PDI was responsible for many of the early CG graphics used to animate logos and other effects in TV commercials.

The next frontier that PDI and its competitors were going for was feature films. The company went head-to-head with George Lucas's visual effects company Industrial Light & Magic (ILM), but lost the bid to create the effects for the movie *Dragonheart*, which, after *Jurassic Park*, became a landmark in the evolution of CG effects.

Marilyn got really good at finding people who had the right chops and the right attitude along with a serious, committed work ethic. She developed hiring protocols and best practices, including the interview system that became a mainstay of HR at the company.

In 1995, Pixar released *Toy Story* through Disney and the industry went into overdrive. PDI was "in play," and the founders were bringing prospective suitors in almost every week to look at the facility and to review the current work in progress.

Later that year, DreamWorks Animation bought a 40 percent stake in the company on its way to acquiring 100 percent a few years later. *Antz*, PDI's first feature animated CG film, was an order of magnitude larger than anything they had done before. Marilyn needed to hire 120 people in five months to ramp up production. It was exhilarating but exhausting. She says it was insane how much she was working—probably sixty to seventy hours per week. She only had one person working with her, and finally, after a year, she was able to hire another two people to begin building what would become the company's HR and recruiting department. PDI's next film, *Shrek*, was already on deck, and the studio was moving to a bigger facility in Palo Alto.

By the time *Antz* was completed, PDI had grown to around 225 employees. DreamWorks began to bring in their own people, so the structure and culture of the merged companies began to change. When *Shrek* opened in the summer of 2001, it became PDI's and DreamWorks's first bona fide smash hit, and Marilyn found herself shuttling back and forth to DreamWorks headquarters in Glendale much more often. With her expertise in finding talented CG artists and programmers, Marilyn was named head of studio recruiting for both campuses, leading teams at both locations.

But despite this outward success, Marilyn was increasingly unhappy. Perhaps it was burnout, but she was feeling increasingly at odds with the supervising leadership at the PDI location. Finally, around the beginning of 2003, she decided to resign. She felt that she had done all she could as a recruiter and that her career wasn't really progressing. The work had become mechanical and she was looking for a new challenge. Not wanting to lose her, DreamWorks management asked her to come back to them with a proposal: "Tell us what you think we need, and what you could do to make that happen. Let's see if we can work something out."

So Marilyn did some research and some thinking. What she saw was an emerging opportunity to create a university outreach program to seed the next generation of talent for the expanding studio. The goal would be to find the best artistic and technical programs in academia and create ongoing relationships with leading faculty to identify and cultivate talented students and hire them before the competition. DreamWorks enthusiastically approved the plan, and CEO Jeffrey Katzenberg himself signed off.

Marilyn's program became bigger than she ever imagined. Starting with seven colleges and universities in late 2004, the program at its peak was working with over forty-five schools in the U.S. and internationally. It became her signature achievement in her almost two decades with the combined company. The whole experience, and the influence that the young recruits had on the various departments within the company, became a significant win-win for everyone involved.

In 2008, in the wake of the recession, things began to shift. The company foresaw harder economic times ahead. As a standalone, publicly traded animation studio, DWA was having a hard time weathering the ups and downs that larger studios could withstand. The company began to thin out at the top, and departments were being consolidated little by little in order to make decision-making a leaner process.

While DWA's movies were mostly profitable, Wall Street continued to demand more consistent financial results—a hard thing to achieve in Hollywood even in the best economic times. Marilyn understood all this, but she never perceived any of these changes as existential threats. She believed that her long, successful tenure at the company made her secure. "I thought that I could go to the people who had been my supporters, who had had my back, and that wouldn't change. I knew that Jeffrey [Katzenberg] loved me, so I thought I was never going to lose my job."

But she was wrong. "Anyone can lose their job," she observes. "It doesn't matter how good you are, how loyal you are. If you're falling on a line item that needs to be marked out, you're out. It's that simple." Despite her sadness and disappointment at leaving the company, she was heartened that Jeffrey did seek her out on her last day to reassure her that she had done nothing wrong.

After Marilyn was let go, her husband Basil was extremely supportive, but what she didn't realize was that he was also concerned about their future, as his business was also being affected by the new economy. The advertising business was shifting away from the kind of food styling work that had been his mainstay.

For two months, Marilyn had a hard time sleeping and lost a lot of weight. She fell out of her routine, including her regular fitness regimen. Finally, she pulled herself together, got out of bed in the morning, and pushed her way back into her routine, walking or running every single day.

Like many people who are blindsided by a layoff, Marilyn didn't have a current résumé, and putting a new one together was a struggle for her. Not having looked for a job since 1993, she felt as if she'd been living in a career cocoon for twenty years.

Her transition out of the company included access to a management consulting/outplacement firm for coaching and training. The outplacement firm was a mixed bag: tt was very corporate, but the coach who was assigned to her was helpful. She found that visiting the firm's offices in downtown San Francisco helped get her out of the house and back into a flow. Most of the others in the program were over fifty and, like Marilyn, had been fired, downsized, or laid off. It was interesting for her to listen to these people, all qualified, articulate professionals who were also in various states of shock and floundering in their own ways. Most had been in companies for twenty to thirty years and were unprepared for the job market. Everyone was commiserating with everyone else, and it made Marilyn feel as if she was not alone. It was validating for her, and spending time at the outplacement firm helped her put things in perspective.

The coaching sessions were more personal than she expected. The coach knew she wasn't quite ready to get out in the job market; she respected Marilyn's space and her boundaries and didn't push hard. Those sessions were a nonjudgmental and safe place for Marilyn. She needed someone to let her talk through what she was feeling and validate it in a way that didn't make her feel as if she needed to rehash her life story or ponder her childhood traumas. The coach was professional and empathetic and understood what it was like to lose a job.

As Mariliyn was beginning to balance her life again, she got more comfortable with networking. The more she met and talked with people, the more fluid the process became, and she felt as though she was learning a new language.

As she refined her goals, she began to get a clearer sense of what she wanted to do and what she didn't want to do. She knew that she needed community, working and interacting with people. Working from home was not the answer for her.

One of her long-standing relationships was with the executive director of a well-funded educational nonprofit, an organization that was implementing innovative curriculum solutions for schools. She liked what they were doing and believed in their mission. They approached her about a six-month consulting gig that might lead to more. She felt it was worth trying. Their local office was a reasonable commute, and she liked the idea of being able to bond with a new set of colleagues.

Right off the bat, she knew she was in trouble. Everyone in the office seemed to be on their own agendas, and there didn't seem to be much sense of cohesion or communication. She had had only a brief meeting with her direct supervisor before she was hired. Now he didn't seem to register that she had joined the organization; there was no onboarding, no goal-setting.

She took it upon herself to introduce herself to her colleagues and found that two of the board members had not been informed that she was being hired. Worse, they weren't happy about it, and made no bones about it in their meetings with her. It took her a couple of weeks to get a meeting with her supervisor to find out what all this meant. Though he attempted to be positive, she realized that she had been hired as a pawn in a conflict between two organizational factions. After six weeks, seeing no clear path to success, she quit.

Initially, she was shaken by the experience. The fact that it didn't work out revived all of her doubts about her abilities and about her career: "Maybe it's my fault," she thought. But she decided to keep looking, theorizing that she would need to kiss a few frogs to find her princely job. She also learned a number of important takeaways from the experience. It reinforced the notion that she did want to work collaboratively in an office with other people. She realized that she hadn't asked the right questions going in—questions like "How does your board work?", "Who has final say?", "Can I see an org chart?", "Can I read the job description?", "What are the expected/desired outcomes?", and "What budget has been allocated to this project?"

If she had asked these questions, it might have shortcut the whole process and helped her to avoid a mistake.

At the next opportunity, she did get all of that information. On paper, the job was terrific. Marilyn was approached by an engineer she had worked with years earlier to join a technology startup that was doing leading-edge work and which was very well-funded by top Silicon Valley venture capitalists.

The salary was right, the benefits were right, the company culture was right. The job description, however, was not. The position was very similar to the recruiting job she had done at PDI in the 1990s. But she didn't want to do recruiting, particularly because she understood the challenge of finding talented technical staff in the midst of an extremely competitive shortage of sophisticated talent. She knew that she could do the job and eventually hire more HR staff to take over the recruiting work. But it would once again mean sixty- to seventy-hour weeks as well as a commute lasting more than an hour each way. So she felt as if she was walking out of the frying pan into the fire. As upbeat, welcoming, and progressive as the company and the management were, she also knew that anything can happen in the startup world, and that her long-term plans could easily be derailed by the wrong sale or the wrong takeover.

She didn't sleep for a couple of days. She hated having to turn down a great job at a time when she really needed one. But she also felt determined that she was not going to make a bad decision that would end up compromising two of her foremost concerns. So she did turn it down, much to the consternation of many of her friends. But she knew that she was making the right decision.

Job feelers continued to come in, but they were off-base, out of the state, or out of the country. She kept networking and met people at all the top tech companies, at the VC firms, and others. She had a lot more conversations, and while they didn't seem to go anywhere, she did feel that she was continuing to define her intentions and the scope of what she wanted to do. She kept thinking that whatever the next step was going to be, it would not be an obvious choice. And that's exactly what happened.

As I've mentioned, when Marilyn was laid off at DWA, Basil had been concerned about his own career situation. So when Marilyn lost her job, Basil decided that he needed to find a job that included health insurance. He got a job with a large commercial food-service provider, pivoting back to working in a kitchen, which he hadn't done in over twenty years. He became head of food services at the local elementary school, minutes away from their house in the East Bay.

One day, after Basil had been at the school for about ten months, he came home with an unusual proposition. One of their neighbors was a teacher who had been assigned to Basil's school. She had mentioned to him that they were looking for an assistant kindergarten teacher, and had asked whether Marilyn might be interested. Her immediate response was, "What do I know about kids or about elementary education?" But Basil persisted: "I'm having fun. . . . It could be interesting."

She talked with their neighbor, who told her, "If you take the job you'll be there to help the teacher. You're not making curriculum decisions. I just think that given who you are, and what you like doing, it might be worthwhile." She urged Marilyn to meet with the principal. He turned out to be a great guy. Marilyn enjoyed the conversation and felt comfortable at the school. But when she went to actually meet the teacher and see the classroom, it was unexpectedly magical: "Everything about that room was interactive—the colors, the sense of life. Things were going on in there! I haven't had kids, so I had never been in classroom like that. It blew me away."

She figured she had nothing to lose. It was just eight miles from her house. The job didn't pay a lot, but it was at least something. And it was only twenty hours per week, which left her plenty of time to continue her job search, meet new people, and continue to network.

Marilyn has been enjoying her unforeseen gig. "It's been a trip! Really interesting in ways that I wasn't expecting. The kids are learning how to learn. That's fascinating to me. I feel like I'm, in a positive way, an enabler. I enable people to be the best they can be and set them up to succeed. It's like setting up these little people to be their best at being sponges. They're amazing! I'm doing it now with the kids, but also with the teacher—she's awesome! And it feels like I'm working to be a strong support for her, which helps her be better at what she does."

The unconditional love from the kids has also been wonderful and unexpected. They jump up when Marilyn arrives and really like her. She's learning a lot from them as well and feels a great sense of responsibility. Her students' parents, she says, "are dropping their whole world off at the front door. I take that incredibly seriously." She loves the variety of the experience. No two days are ever the same. And the kids crack her up—she loves the wisdom and the humor that comes out of their mouths.

Ironically, as someone who has spent most of her career looking for talent, developing talent, and putting the right people together to leverage their talent, she's doing the same thing in that elementary school, except at a different and arguably much more formative level.

It has also unexpectedly opened up a new dimension in Marilyn's relationship with Basil. In thirty-seven years, they had never worked in proximity to each other. She wasn't home a lot in the two decades at PDI/DWA. So working in the same place is fun. The kids, of course, figured it out. They asked her right off the bat: "Do you live with the chef?"

For now, they're both trying to stay very much in the moment. They can't say how long they'll be doing this, but for right now, they're making it work. She's continuing to look at opportunities on the outside, but if she's going to take on another gig, it will have to be thoroughly compatible in substance and scheduling to the life she and Basil have built around the school.

Her final takeaway is typically Marilyn: focused, but self-deprecating: "When I'm there, I'm all in, but when I'm gone, I'm gone. I don't think about it! That is amazing. I have so much more time, because I don't take work home and don't commute. Sometimes I feel guilty, but then I think: what is wrong with me!?"

Chapter 7

JULIE MURPHY:
FINALLY DARING TO DITCH
THE CORPORATE CAREER

JULIE MURPHY'S EXECUTIVE CAREER was full of job changes and new opportunities, but she never believed that she could have it all: a career that combined her philosophical and spiritual side with her command of business strategy and analysis. In a race against time to keep paying for her daughter's education, she finally came to realize that the career she wanted was really just a step away.

Part of her challenge was needing to overcome the limiting belief that she was not cut out for an entrepreneurial or freelance career—despite coming from a family where solo practitioners were the norm. Her father had his own law firm, her brother had his own architecture/design firm, and her mother had owned a travel agency. She also needed to figure out how to reconcile the risk and uncertainty of launching her own business with the tenuous security she got from enduring toxic work environments as an executive. As accomplished and smart as Julie was, she refused for many years to let go of dysfunctional environments. Her key reframe was the gradual acceptance and incorporation of her spiritual and mindfulness studies as integral pillars of her career versus seeing them as external sanctuaries that stood apart from her work.

Julie was always an extremely motivated, self-directed young woman. Growing up and going to college and law school in the New

York City area, she passed two bar exams and was delighted to get the law job she wanted. But about ten months after she began practicing, she woke up one morning wondering, "Is this it?" She had a gnawing sense that even though she had hit all of her milestones, there had to be something more than the work she was doing.

This was the beginning of Julie's spiritual quest. "I think a lot of my reinventing myself over and over again is because of that sense that there's got to be more for me in this lifetime," she says.

This is not to say that her work as a lawyer had no purpose—quite the contrary. Julie had gone to law school so that she could represent battered women, and that is exactly what she did for the six years that she practiced law. It was very fulfilling work that changed people's lives for the better. Still, she felt unsatisfied.

Thinking she might be happier in a different environment, she began applying to other firms and even came close to taking one position. Instead, she decided to stay home with her two-year-old daughter for a while, trying to figure out her next career move.

After about two years at home, she saw an ad for a computer programing course and signed up, not quite knowing what to expect but intrigued by the idea of using her analytical skills in a new way. Out of the approximately fifty people who had showed up to learn about the course, she and a handful of other people were asked to stay and learn more about this program.

She wound up taking a six-month course in mainframe computer programming. While she found it challenging, she was one of a handful of students who were good enough to successfully complete the program. She was offered a position as a systems analyst at AT&T and worked there for about nine months. Then a friend offered her a job with a small computer consulting company in New York City, where she helped the company manage the deployment of large-scale systems, mostly customer relationship management (CRM) applications, to their clients. She really got into the work and enjoyed it quite a lot. In addition to the deployments, she was also training employees, which added an entirely new portfolio of skills.

A national youth development nonprofit found Julie's résumé on Monster.com and offered her a position as head of project management. The job and the timing were perfect for her: the nonprofit had just hired a new CEO, and Julie would have the chance to help her implement a new business strategy. "I couldn't have walked in the door at a better time," she says. For the next seven or eight years, Julie helped to roll out first the national strategy and then helped affiliates create local strategies that was nationally aligned. She got to work closely with an expert consultant, a former corporate CEO who had been teaching Columbia University business school.

Julie's portfolio expanded to include change management, strategy execution, and leadership development. The CEO, "a leftover hippie" in Julie's words, kept throwing her into new experiences and helping her flesh out ideas that she really cared about, all pivoting off of an overall focus on strategy. "I got exposed to so many things," Julie marvels. Her relationship with the CEO was very hands-off. The CEO would swoop in every few months, inspire Julie to take on another evolutionary and eye-opening project, and then go away to let her figure it out.

When the CEO left the company, things quickly changed. With the new leadership, Julie felt that it was time to think about what was next. She stuck around for another year, continuing to do her work and trying to stay under the radar amidst significant change. It was a difficult year for everyone at the organization. At some point, a comprehensive restructure was announced and the feeling within the organization was one of fear. People kept their heads down waiting for the layoffs to begin. Julie saw that morale was negatively impacted. Most frustrating, Julie's skills were no longer being utilized.

In an attempt to make working there more palatable for herself and her team, Julie instituted what became a game-changing set of mindfulness practices, using techniques for centering the mind and clearing distractions that she had picked up from her meditation practice and other meditators. She brought a little bell to meetings and would ring it at the beginning and the end of each meeting so that the group could focus and take a quiet minute of reflection to clear their minds. Julie implemented "check-ins" and "check-outs" at the beginning and end of each meeting for people to share where they were and what was on their mind. This practice helped build cohesion and empathy as well as helped people become more present for each other and the topics covered in the meeting.

This simple practice created controversy. But team members who reacted cynically and impatiently when she first instituted the practice became devoted to it after a few months when they began to realize the benefits. In an otherwise deteriorating corporate environment, Julie began getting requests from other employees to attend her meetings. Her team members began spontaneously offering to help one another out on projects and otherwise support one another's work. Julie's team was a happy, high performing team in an environment that felt unsupportive and ominous.

Julie realized that people wanted to bring their whole selves to work every day rather than sacrificing what made them feel fulfilled for the sake of conformity to a bland, impersonal, factory-like environment. People began to seek her out to talk to her about how they could better integrate their beliefs about wellness and spirituality into their work lives. This experience no doubt contributed to her own quest for an integrated approach to her own fulfillment at work.

Some leaders seemed threatened by the unity and cohesion of Julie's team and made derogatory comments about the practices. Following a few rounds of lay-offs, Julie decided it was time to leave the organization and negotiated her exit, even though she was offered several jobs in the new structure.

She left at the end of 2013 after ten years with the organization. As part of her settlement, she was kept on for a few months to write a report documenting and analyzing a specific company initiative that had occurred earlier in her tenure. She was the last remaining executive with working knowledge of the initiative, as everyone else had either left or been fired, and this project gave her the opportunity to decompress from her bad experience and to ponder where she was going to go from there.

Just before completing the report, she attended a weekend meditation retreat. She realized in a flash of insight that the only way forward in her career was to combine her business acumen with her spiritual life—not to try to find a conventional job that would leave her room for a separate spiritual practice.

The very next day, Julie was finalizing the report when she saw a blog post by Daniel Goleman, the psychologist best known for making emotional intelligence a common business and leadership concept. The post referenced an upcoming training program called Search Inside Yourself for people interested in teaching mindfulness and emotional intelligence in business. The program was created and tested at Google and now was being brought into the world by the Search Inside Yourself Leadership Institute. The training was highly competitive and would take place all of 2014 in San Francisco. Julie realized that this could be the perfect next step for her.

Everyone in her family thought this sounded like a great idea. With only five days to go before the application deadline, she recorded a video covering her experience using the bell with her work team and describing the positive effects of using small but significant practices as means to improve relationships, morale, and productivity within an organization. She was accepted into the program.

After the Christmas holidays, as she prepared to shuttle back and forth to San Francisco every few months, Julie began looking for a new job in earnest. She wound up taking an internal consulting position focusing on change management with a telecom company. Her rationale was that she saw herself eventually consulting on her own, and this would be a good opportunity to test the waters and lay down some approaches and best practices that she could use down the line.

The Search Inside Yourself course, spread out over the remainder of 2014, became the benchmark experience that would support her eventual decision to go out on her own: "That class was a game-changer for me. What I had been saying for the last couple of years . . . was that I had to find my people, and when I got to San Francisco . . . [these] were the kind of people that I wanted to be surrounded by."

Unfortunately, her new job quickly proved to be even more problematic than her last one. She had landed in a cutthroat political environment that was completely at odds with the values-driven leadership principles she was studying in San Francisco. Julie would come back from classes feeling open and positive, but go back to work in a fear-based workplace.

To counteract the negativity, she would get up extra early to meditate, listen to uplifting podcasts on her way to work, and keep a Gratitude Journal to channel the frustrations and keep a positive outlook during the day. She also shared elements of the Search Inside Yourself program with members of her department, who told her it was inspiring and effective. Still, the overall atmosphere continued to deteriorate: "I was in this 'boot camp' of how to stay positive, and it really wasn't working."

Despite the toxicity she had to deal with every day, Julie stayed at the telecom. When I asked her why, she said that she had a crippling fear of leaving and starting out on her own. Her daughter was also in her last year of college, and despite having enough money in the bank to cover the year, she felt vulnerable financially.

Many people find themselves in the same situation as Julie. You get used to the environment; you get used to the people. You have memories and shared experiences together, and you identify yourself with the company, however dysfunctional it may be. It is also extremely difficult to juggle a job and your outside responsibilities while thinking about planning a new move that could very well disrupt your life. So, like many people, Julie gritted her teeth and soldiered on.

In December 2014, at the last Search Inside Yourself weekend, Julie shared her misgivings and her fears with others in the class. They tried to reassure her, but even their positive support couldn't alleviate the inner panic that she was experiencing. As 2015 started and the situation at the telecom got worse, she continued to debate whether or not she should leave, but her concerns about money held her back. She at least wanted to see her daughter graduate from college before making any life-changing decisions.

After fourteen months, and just four days after her daughter's graduation, much to Julie's relief, the company laid her off with a very healthy severance package. She realized that now would finally be the perfect time to launch her own business. She was further encouraged by some of her team members at the telecom. They were grateful for the uplifting concepts and prescriptions that she had shared from the Search Inside Yourself program, and they expressed their confidence in her ability to take these practices out into the world.

Since leaving the telecom in the middle of 2015, Julie has been building her private consulting practice as a certified mindfulness teacher and leadership development consultant.

She has had to push back against the fear that was always holding her back from having her own business: "I had this sense that other people know how this works, but I don't have a clue . . . that I don't know how to do this; that there's this secret formula that everyone knows." She has also realized that conquering her fear was very much a question of attitude: "We all go down into fear from time to time, but if you watch it, you can manage your fears and emotions." She uses her training and her techniques to hold the vision every day for how she wants her practice to grow.

In the beginning, she had a hard time thinking of herself as someone who could build a business: "When people talk about business development, I break out in a cold sweat—I don't really know what that means." But she has slowly worked through that limiting belief, based in part on hearing how one of her fellow alumni from the Search Inside Yourself program approaches her business. This woman said that instead of looking at developing your business as being a "hunter" who must seek out and track down customers, you can look at yourself as a "magnet"—someone who shares herself and her solutions with the world. When you are a magnet, people gravitate to you to learn more and ask you to help them integrate your solutions into their businesses. That was a key reframe for Julie, as she saw that approach as being more natural for her and more compatible with her philosophy and way of life.

Julie has been in the process of developing and pitching her consulting practice in whatever way she can, doing presentations and speaking gigs "with the hope that enough people are going to get to know me as the mindfulness person in central New Jersey, and that it's going to take hold that way."

And she has experienced a wealth of serendipity since she started her business. "I pinch myself sometimes. I keep wondering: how did that just happen?" She also works with gratitude and embracing what comes her way as a central strategy for her work, just being in a state of agreement—a state of "yes." Julie pretty much says yes to any idea, any suggestion. Meet a new person? Yes. Attend a new meeting? Yes. "I keep saying 'yes' to everything that comes my way."

As a result, good things are happening. Julie has gotten known in her area and now gets calls from companies who are interested in bringing in mindfulness for leadership development, stress reduction, resilience, and productivity. She is often introduced to people who miraculously open doors or ask to collaborate with her. Julie has also been given work through several larger consulting firms both in the US and in Europe. She recently got hired to teach mindfulness and resilience to wealth managers in London, Mumbai, and Beijing and had an amazing around the world adventure while teaching what she loves.

A wonderful bi-product of this journey is that Julie has met amazing people while teaching, networking, and exploring business opportunities. She has found a whole new circle of friends and colleagues that share similar values and are committed to personal practice. Julie even has a monthly mindfulness dinner with three friends who are all trying to bring mindfulness into their companies and organizations.

Julie laughs about all this, because it just seems so random, but, as she says, "I never question anything because I feel like the universe has something in store for me, and I just have to keep moving forward. Saying yes to opportunities and surrendering to the process has become a way of life."

Clearly, Julie is the magnet that her colleague was talking about. She is presenting something that is clear and authentic. It may not be for everyone, but for those who are aligned with her, what she can provide for people is highly attractive and valuable. Julie talks about having wanted to find her tribe for a long time. Now that is beginning to happen. Anyone who comes up to her at a gathering where Julie is speaking or simply attending is automatically one of her tribe in her eyes.

Julie credits her mindfulness practice for the success of her reinvention. "It really got me in touch with my emotional state moment to moment, and before that I'd been pretty cut off from it. But now, if I feel like I'm getting worried or scared, I go back and I meditate, I journal, I do all sorts of things to shift, because I know that my emotional state is always changing and that I have some control over it. So I think my personal practices have made a huge difference in my being able to stay optimistic for my future."

Chapter 8.

DAN GOETZ: DISCOVERING THE INNER ENTREPRENEUR

AT A TIME IN LIFE WHEN MANY PEOPLE are supposed to be pulling back from their careers, Dan Goetz discovered that taking on more responsibility through owning a business actually liberated him, turning the loss of a long-held job into a fruitful exercise in fulfillment and success. As Dan's experience attests, when the world sends you the message that your skills and knowledge are no longer valuable, a few key reframes and a willingness to look beyond your prior experience may hold the key to a much more successful and sustainable future.

Dan's story also highlights the value of listening—specifically the power of peer mentorship and participating in so-called mastermind groups, both of which can be great ways to leverage feedback from like-minded professionals. (As you'll see in Part III of this book, Listening is one of the crucial steps in the Boomer Reinvention methodology.)

Dan was an operations guy who, over ten years, had worked his way up to the top role at a Southern California manufacturer of ultra-violet radiation water and air purification devices. Dan was one of a four-person senior management team working for the owner of this privately held company. One day, Dan scheduled a meeting with the owner to ask for more engagement and more guidance for the senior team. In response, the owner surprised Dan by appointing him president of the company. In retrospect, Dan saw that the owner had been waiting for someone to emerge from the pack and take initiative. Once Dan stepped forward, the owner's plan was to move up to a chairman role and let Dan take over the day-to-day leadership at the company.

At first, Dan felt somewhat at a loss in his new role. While he was pleased to have been promoted, he still needed guidance and support. A friend referred him to Vistage, a national organization that conducts mastermind business groups for senior executives, run by former senior executives, CEOs, and business coaches. Small groups meet monthly to support governance issues, operations, strategy, and the personal challenges that owners and chief executives of small- to medium-sized businesses face every day.

Dan participated in a Vistage group for five years. The feedback and support from this group helped him run the company better. But as you'll see, it also helped him through his transition out of the company, setting him up for a more entrepreneurial path ahead.

Dan had always seen himself as a "hired gun," never as a business owner. He had spent his career happily working for others, working hard and doing well, but never dreaming of having his own business. Looking back, he sees that he always had the ingredients to be a leader and to step into that kind of role, but never really stopped to consider it. He also assumed that someone in the CEO role would have to be quite different from himself—someone more dynamic and gifted, with new ideas for products and business models. So Dan felt that a supportive role as head of operations was all that he was capable of playing.

The Vistage group exposed him to the entrepreneurial mindset, and he found himself willing to consider the idea that maybe there could be more for him out there than being a hired gun. He gradually became comfortable in his new role as company president, and he began to enjoy the expanded responsibility.

When the company founder passed away in 2006, his two sons inherited the company. They were not businessmen, and neither one had ever worked at the company. The sons signed Dan to a three-year employment agreement. Over these three years, Dan trained one of the sons in the company's business and operations, half believing that the son would still want Dan around to run the business. But when the agreement expired in 2009, the son did not extend the agreement and, instead, let Dan go. Dan probably should have seen it coming, but, by his own admission, he had grown complacent. So he had no contingency plans.

It took Dan around six weeks to get to the stage where he felt comfortable talking about himself, making calls, and starting to pitch his talents to people. The most important thing for him was to learn to "get past the steps of denial and grieving and all that very very fast . . . because it just slows you down. You've got to get a positive attitude going very quickly." He knew that no one really wanted to commiserate with him, and that wallowing in self-pity wouldn't get him anywhere. He needed to get past the sense of loss and get to a place where he was willing and able to take back control of his life.

He had been attentive to following the "networking mantra," as he calls it—making sure to stay in touch with people who understood and supported him, and who could be helpful to him in shaping his future career. He wasn't too focused on seeking out job postings to apply to, opting instead to rely on his relationships to guide him to meeting new people and planting the seeds for an eventual position that would be the right fit.

Initially, the effectiveness of his networking efforts was, in his word, "dramatic." People were taking his calls, and he built up a certain amount of traction. There is no doubt in his mind about the value of focusing on one's network: "It works. It doesn't work overnight. But it works!"

The problem was that it was taking too long. He spent almost a year networking without finding a new position, and in the process he burned through much of his savings. Making matters worse, the value of his house had tumbled by almost fifty percent because of the recession. Dan felt as if he was running out of time.

For the first four to six months after he left the company, he thought he was going to find another job as president, CEO, or some other senior hired-gun position. But as more time went by, he realized that he needed to try a different approach and expand his mind to consider other options.

Things may have turned around for him because of an epiphany he had about how he was presenting himself. Instead of talking about what role people wanted him to fill, he started asking people what problem they had that they needed solving. The tone of the conversations started to change, and Dan's overtures began to get taken a lot more seriously. Invariably the interview would shift from him having to promote himself and why he was a good candidate, to the company and what the company was trying to achieve and how he could be a solution provider. He never knew where the conversations would end up, but he felt a lot better about the meetings and about himself.

At some point in this process, one of Dan's contacts, a CPA, introduced him to a small team of private equity investors who were turnaround specialists. They had a problem, and the CPA thought that Dan might be the guy who could solve it for them.

This firm bought "distressed equity" companies—companies that were struggling to stay in business—and brought in new management with strategies to turn them around. They were interested in having Dan play a leadership role at one of these distressed businesses. Dan found this challenge intriguing. "All of sudden, I found myself still in a hired-gun position, but I was going to be a minority owner in a potential distressed equity turnaround." He spent a couple of days walking around the company they were looking to fix, meeting with people and evaluating the opportunity to see if he could diagnose and solve their problem.

He then sat down with the investors and presented his analysis and his game plan. His tactical solution: firing the company's largest customer. The company had been losing money on this customer but was too scared to deal with the problem. Dan told them that they had to either raise their prices or cut the customer loose.

The investors called Dan the next day and told him they wanted him to come on board. The company followed Dan's plan by cutting ties with the money-losing customer. Firing that customer changed the company's focus from volume to profitability. Dan was able to change their thinking. Within forty-five days of starting, Dan was able to turn the company around from a $50,000-per-month deficit to a positive cash flow. Within three months, they were making profits of $50,000 per month.

The book value of the company was over $5 million, but the private equity firm had bought it for $800,000. After two years with Dan at the helm, they sold it for $2.4 million—three times what they'd bought it for. Dan got a piece of the sale. He realized that when you put yourself in an ownership role, you benefit from an entirely different reward system. It's not about taking a paycheck home every week. It's about creating value.

That was Dan's big takeaway during this transitional career phase. But while he liked the idea of turning a company around and making something functional and profitable out of something that was failing, he didn't like the "buy it, fix it, flip it" mentality of the distressed equity investors, which didn't fit his values very well. He didn't like the slash-and-burn approach, where employees got fired to make the companies leaner or assets had to be sold to make the balance sheets look better. He got no internal satisfaction from putting people out of work. He saw himself as a more of a long-term value builder.

Dan decided to look more closely at the distressed equity business to see if there was a way of doing it with more integrity He wanted to find partners who would work with him to use the process to promote long-term growth. And he found that there were multiple types of private equity people. So having gone through this experience of putting his toe in the water, Dan was now actually ready to be an owner of a company instead of the hired gun.

Dan sat down with his wife to map out the next step. The timing seemed right for them. Their kids were grown and out of the house. They didn't have anything monumental holding them back from making a change. Dan's wife encouraged him to think big and to pursue something new. After the difficult year they had had after he was let go from his job, she was open to moving somewhere else to start a new life.

Working with a private equity group in Menlo Park, CA, Dan was able to find a takeover target that was the right fit for him. Rather than focusing on flipping companies, this investor group was more interested in buying for the long term and in creating lasting value. This clearly aligned with Dan's values, and the collaboration led to a very successful deal. They bought a manufacturing company in Oregon, where Dan is now the controlling shareholder with 24 percent ownership. Running this company has been a great success, and Dan has taken on an entirely different role that he greatly enjoys: "It has met a lot of internal needs for me. . . . I feel like I could have been an entrepreneur all along and never knew it."

When Dan and his partners bought the company, there was no 401(k) plan for the employees, no life insurance plan, only a very basic medical plan, and infrequent raises. Management was something of a mess. In the three years since, Dan has worked hard to improve the quality of the workplace. He implemented dental, vision, and life insurance benefits, offers educational reimbursement programs, started an annual company picnic, and instituted other community practices and benefits that are totally new. This past year at the picnic, the employees all pitched in and presented Dan with a very expensive Trager BBQ smoker. He was floored—and almost in tears. They told him, "This company is completely different since you've been here." No one has left the company in two years. And the business has grown from $7.2 million to $12.5 million in sales.

As an owner, Dan is thinking completely differently. He's looking at the difference between growth and value. He's looking for ways to increase the value of the enterprise, not just for increased revenue. Different factors come into play, including intellectual property protection, long-term contracts with customers, and protecting, supporting, and retaining talent. He finds it deeply fulfilling to have a hand in developing the culture of the organization and hiring the right kind of people to help accomplish his goals for the company. It represents a totally different kind of internal satisfaction—and a different kind of risk. He has to continually look to himself and assess whether he's doing the right thing for his people and making the right decisions.

To support his leadership, Dan once again turned to Vistage, joining a local group in Oregon. He is bouncing issues off of this group, including strategic-level decisions about the future of his company. But he knows that ultimately, whatever course he chooses is totally his responsibility, and he's fine with that: "The decisions are all mine to make."

In joining the Vistage group, Dan finds himself dealing with issues on a different level. "I'm looking for feedback about the potential impact on the future of the business, as opposed to more tactical questions that

I was dealing with as an employee." He is also getting great benefit out of interacting with the younger business-owners in the group—CEOs in their mid-thirties to mid-forties who are tech savvy and in tune with the millennials who are coming up just after them. Dan finds their new ideas and methods illuminating. For example, a forty-year-old entrepreneur who is running a branding agency spends a lot of time optimizing the office space for a work layout that will promote creativity and collaboration. She has a different take on staffing and compensation packages, and how to onboard entry-level kids coming into the company. She's also dealing with what Dan considers an alarmingly high turnover rate, but he understands that this is due to the attitudes of her millennial workforce. Seeing it through her eyes gives him a better understanding of how the workforce is changing, and how he can better address the needs of his own younger employees. "They've got to figure out if these are people they want to hold onto, and how to create an environment, and a compensation package, and a benefits package, that entices these people to stay. I learn interesting things from [these owners], and it's a different set of problems from what I [used to] deal with."

As the "sage" in the room, Dan has had a chance to be a mentor to these younger entrepreneurs. This is particularly valuable when someone brings up an issue that he has been through, perhaps multiple times, and he can really help walk them through the possible solutions, itemizing the steps to resolve it. It feels good to be able to provide that kind of support.

For example, the CEO of an events-planning company who works with large Oregon-based tech companies was having difficulty retaining employees who were constantly being poached by his clients. He was the victim of his own success, impressing clients with large, well-managed, glitzy events, but then losing staff to these same companies who wanted to manage more events in-house. Dan asked, "What have you done to create an environment where your staff knows what their future looks like with your company? How are you taking a personal interest in their future, and helping them to get where they want to go in their careers?" He suggested that the company present a path for individual staffers that addressed the things that they want while also outlining for them how staying with the organization could take them to an entirely new place or new level in their career. He laughs: "I can't tell you with great certainty that it made a profound impact in their HR department, but the [CEO's response] was very positive to me!"

Interacting with younger owners has definitely influenced Dan's own management style for the better. Dan was used to working onsite during conventional business hours. Like most boomers, he grew up with the idea that in order to get work done, you have to come in to the office. Now he has learned that younger professionals want to work at all kinds of hours, not just nine to five. So he has come to accept the need for a workplace that caters to the ways that employees want to work, not forcing employees to work according to the way management says they have to work. In response, he has built a technology infrastructure to communicate outside of the walls of the office, outside of conventional business hours, and which allows people the flexibility to do the kind of work that they do. Most importantly, he understands that this flexibility is not an indulgence; it is really a strategic way to maximize employees' productivity and give them the opportunity to do their best work.

The new infrastructure cost money to install and costs money to maintain, "but now that I've seen it at work, I was foolish to put up any resistance," Dan says. Projects are moving forward faster than ever before. And even the older workers have adapted and are taking advantage of the flexibility and empowerment that the new systems and paradigms allow.

Dan advises those who are embarking on a career reinvention to describe in writing a script for their career, and to be specific about what their ideal job would look like. What responsibilities would they want and what would they want to avoid? What is their long-term objective— not for the business, but for their own life and well-being?

Dan's takeaway is that boomers faced with career uncertainty need to take charge and be proactive, and start gathering experiences, meeting people, and researching new ideas with a beginner's mind. He doesn't think it matters what kind of business you've been in, or what kind of business you think you want to go into. There are many ways to gather real, immediate, and practical information on whether a new career path could work for you.

He suggests, for example, shadowing someone in a role or a business you think might be an option for you. Start having conversations with people—in person through referrals, or online through LinkedIn—to find out about what they're doing. Build the relationship to the point where you could actually visit them onsite and spend a morning or an afternoon. Getting up close to a job is going to give you a much better sense of whether it could work for you. It's a better option than reading about it or talking about it. "Anything that you can do to get close to your idea is great!" Dan also recommends volunteering as a way of testing your ideas in some types of careers.

Dan warns boomers who are hesitating about starting their reinvention: don't wait. Don't be complacent about the potential disruptions you see coming your way. Dan had three years in his previous company before he was fired, but he didn't prepare for that scenario. "So I sit back today and say that I missed three years of an opportunity to be in a better place. … There's no fixing that problem, [but] I'm just happy the way it landed."

Dan's biggest lesson: "You can't re-create the old reality. You have to create a new reality with more control." He feels that even if you have a plan, and you're working your plan, you also have to keep your eyes open for new directions and to seize new opportunities. When someone asked him in the early days after he was let go, "Why don't you buy your own company?" he realized that he had never thought about that before. That question planted the seed for what has become his dream reinvention.

Today Dan has different concerns. At age sixty-four, he is being more discerning about the kinds of problems he is willing to tackle and the goals he wants to set for himself and the company. In his hired-gun days, he made his decisions by looking over his shoulder at his management, calibrating his commitments, and setting the bar at a level where he could be successful from their point of view. Whether it was hiring staff, deploying resources, or hitting a specific profit target, the ultimate consequences of his decisions were moderated by the company owner, not by him.

Today, he is that owner—and he is loving every minute of it.

Chapter 9.

VALERIE RAMSEY: STAYING POSITIVE NO MATTER WHAT

VALERIE RAMSEY IS ONE OF THE MOST gloriously positive people I have ever met. You would probably need to be in order to raise six kids and then, at age fifty-three, decide to jump into the work-force. Today, at age seventy-six, she continues to thrive as a magazine executive and public speaker—and, believe it or not, as a working model.

Valerie's reinvention is a short course in using personal drive and motivation to overcome fear, a lack of preparation, and personal challenges to forge ahead and attain your goals. It may not be an example that everyone can follow, but it illustrates that it is possible to go from zero to sixty in a short amount of time (four years) and then continue to thrive despite the unforeseen challenges that life can throw your way. She was motivated by the inspirational words of Eleanor Roosevelt: "You gain strength, courage, and confidence by every experience in which you really stop to look fear in the face. . . . You must do the thing you think you cannot do."

Valerie is just on the older side of the boomer generation. She came of age at a time just before the modern women's movement, when most women put aside careers to get married and raise a family. Valerie's independence and resilience may have something to do with the fact that her mother was an executive with Intercontinental Hotels who traveled a lot, setting an example for her daughter that was unusual for the time.

But perhaps in reaction to the somewhat lonely life she had as a child, Valerie dreamed of having the ideal Brady Bunch family. When she married her college sweetheart, Wally, she settled in for the long haul (they're stilled married today, fifty-five years later). They moved to Greenwich, CT, where Wally taught at Greenwich Country Day School, and Valerie delivered her six kids by the time she was thirty. Being at home with her large family was all she wanted in her twenties and thirties. But then what?

When Valerie was fifty-three, Wally was offered a teaching position near Monterey, CA, and the family moved to the West Coast. After her youngest graduated from high school and went off to college, Valerie decided that she wanted a challenge, the opportunity to travel, and a more expansive life. No longer saddled with the same level of responsibilities at home, she decided that her goal, inspired in part by her mother's career, was to become a hotel concierge.

The Pebble Beach Resort immediately captured her imagination. She knew it well, and even though she and Wally were not golfers, she had visited the resort many times over the years, even before moving to the area. She loved the ambiance of the place. During all of the years she had visited the resort, it had never occurred to her that she might someday work there. But now she decided that if she had a choice as to where she would love to work, it would be at Pebble Beach.

When she started talking to friends and family about wanting to go to work, a woman she knew suggested that she apply for an administrative assistant position at the resort. Valerie thought, "That's impossible. I did typing and shorthand years ago, but they'd never hire me." But Valerie's friend "pushed me out the door, and gave me the courage to go to HR."

She laughs: "So here comes this fifty-something woman with no current experience and no résumé." In her first meeting, they had Valerie fill out the usual application forms, which only confirmed what little experience she had. She was hoping to find some sort of position that would get her on track for the concierge desk, but all they were willing to do was offer her a job behind the counter at the resort's pro shop, and they probably expected her to turn up her nose at such an idea. She would be selling golf balls and working alongside mostly college kids on their summer break.

But Valerie had no ego and no qualms about the job. The idea that she was old enough to be the mother of her new colleagues never seemed to come into play. Having a good sense of humor and a willingness to help out made a big difference for Valerie in working with younger colleagues: "If you go in with that kind of attitude, nobody cares how old you are."

Having gotten her proverbial foot in the door, she next looked at the different departments to figure out where she might find an opportunity to get out of the pro shop. Since being a concierge required training and background that she wasn't going to easily get, she shifted her focus to more attainable targets. She didn't think she was right for sales, catering, or conference management, but she loved the idea of public relations and marketing.

This was the early 1990s, and she knew that everyone in an administrative capacity needed at least basic computer skills. Valerie had none, so she went to the local community college where she took a great business-skills class that schooled her in the hardware and software and gave her a bit more confidence. She redrafted her résumé, made friends, worked hard, and bided her time. After a few months, a position opened up at Pebble Beach's corporate office for an assistant in the marketing department. She applied, thinking, "Oh my gosh, if I get this it will be a miracle," but they interviewed her twice and offered her the job.

For the next three years, Valerie worked as an executive assistant. She was constantly learning new skills, mostly just by doing what needed to get done. There were only five or six people in the department, so there was always plenty to do. She became the assistant to both the senior vice president and the director of marketing. Additionally, the public relations manager and the resort's graphic designer sat next to her in the office. They produced newsletters and signage, managed events, posted press trips, and cleared credentials for media covering golf tournaments. Valerie found herself in the thick of all of the events at the resort, including the celebrated annual Pebble Beach Concours d'Elegance car show, the AT&T Pebble Beach Pro-Am, and five U.S. Open Championships. Her outgoing personality was clearly a good fit for her role in the department, and she became an indispensable member of the team.

She particularly enjoyed working with the PR manager and often asked to help out on her projects, thinking that if this woman ever moved on, she would love to take over that position. This woman was very forthcoming with her, and mentored her unofficially in the PR business. Sure enough, after Valerie had been in the department for almost four years, the PR manager told Valerie that she was going to quit to accept another position. Valerie was surprised, but then asked her what she thought about Valerie applying to move into her position. The woman smiled and said, "Go for it!"

So Valerie went to the senior vice president of marketing that afternoon and asked for the job. He thought about it for a moment, smiled, and told her, "Okay, you got it!" Just like that. He had worked with her and seen what she could do over the past four years. It did make sense that someone from the inside would be a perfect fit for that position. And of course Valerie had spent a significant amount of time supporting the PR manager, so it would really be a seamless transition.

Switching to an actual corporate job at age fifty-seven was indeed daunting. Valerie had no formal preparation to be a full-time PR exec. No matter how familiar she was with the operation, she was now on the line.

It had taken her four years to get the kind of job she had initially wanted, so she was pumped up and excited. On her first official day, Cadillac was coming to the resort to shoot a commercial. She also had to manage a special executive event that had been booked—not an unusual day at a first-class resort like Pebble Beach.

But Valerie was very nervous, and got up super early to make sure she was on top of everything. On the way into work, she slipped and broke her ankle. Somehow she got through the day. But the day after that, hobbling around on crutches and in her cast, she received worse news: her doctor called to tell her that the results of her recent ob-gyn exam had come in positive. Valerie had cancer.

She was scheduled for a hysterectomy the following week. Before the surgery, her friends and family were obviously very worried about her. Should she quit her job and just focus on her health? But quitting was never an option for her; she had created a new life for herself, and it meant too much to her. Her boss was completely understanding and supportive and told her to take the time she needed.

Coming out of surgery the following week, Valerie got yet another piece of bad news. Further tests had revealed that she had a condition known as viral cardio myopathy, a gradual weakening of the heart muscle for which there is no cure. In most cases, the condition worsens, leading to the need for a heart transplant. Nevertheless, Valerie decided that she would not only survive the condition, but that she would prevail and make the second half of her life even better than the first half. Today it has been almost twenty years since her diagnosis.

During her two-month recovery, the prospect of getting back to work became the light at the end of the tunnel, motivating her to get well, to get stronger, and to come back with a completely renewed sense of herself and what she could do. Her recovery was mental and emotional as much as physical. She surrounded herself with family, friends, and other positive people to help reinforce her certainty that she would be okay. She took the attitude that everybody has something to cope with as they age, so her predicament was not any different from the norm. Therefore, she was just going to accept her condition and be grateful for each day. Her health challenges seem to have reinforced and amplified her sense of purpose and determination.

Valerie also felt very supported by the culture at the resort. In retrospect, she thinks that some of that had to do with how well she fit in with the marketing and PR department. Had she been in sales or another department, she doesn't think she would have necessarily had the same experience. Overall, though, the company seems to be one of the last bastions of old-school corporate values; many of the people she worked with there in the 1990s up until the time she left in 2008 are still working at the company and still in touch with her.

Her big takeaway from her experience finding a foothold at Pebble Beach was that she was right to have accepted that entry-level position in the pro shop despite being "too old" for it. "If you know in your gut that the job is going to grow into something meaningful," she says, then it is smart to just go for it and look for a way up from there. It's a message that reinforces that idea of the beginner's mind. It's also a perfect example of the Reframing process at work—one of the crucial steps in the Boomer Reinvention methodology, as we'll discuss in Part III of this book.

Valerie sees the interpersonal aspects of a job as more important for older workers. They are likely to be under greater pressure to deliver not just on what they do, but on how they do it and how they relate to their colleagues. She worked hard to walk the line between being open and friendly and being *too* open and *too* friendly. She tried to be extremely professional but really nice at the same time—an exemplary team player. Valerie feels that a certain amount of openness, humility, and interest in others will go a long way toward helping you integrate into the organization and mitigate some of the bias or defensiveness that you might encounter as an older worker.

Valerie says she has not encountered very much ageism. It seems as if she bulldozed her way through any ageism that might have been in her way by, as she says, making friends instead. She never stopped to wonder about how people felt about her because she was in her fifties. She felt that her attitude was much more important than her chronology.

One day, after about ten years at the resort, Valerie was overseeing a photo shoot on the property when she was approached by a Hollywood producer staying at the resort. This man was convinced that despite her age, Valerie was the perfect candidate for a modeling career, and he commissioned a photo shoot to prove it. The producer helped Valerie get signed to a Los Angeles modeling agency, and her modeling career took off.

Modeling was lots of fun, but not something that she wanted to interfere with her real job at Pebble Beach. So for the next five years she juggled her PR duties and intermittent photo shoots until she ultimately decided it was time to leave her job. In the interim, Valerie's dual career had attracted a good deal of media attention and TV appearances. She had also been inspired to write her first book, Gracefully: Looking and Being Your Best at Any Age. The book created additional career opportunities for her as a public speaker.

When Valerie left Pebble Beach, she made sure to publicly acknowledge the CEO of the resort, thanking him for giving her an opportunity to begin a new career at age fifty-three. On the theory that you never know where life is going to lead you, Valerie wanted to make sure to leave the company on good terms.

This is a particularly important issue for boomers who are facing downsizing or layoffs, or who are ambivalent about retiring from their jobs. Leaving on good terms is a way to rise above any bad feelings. Even if it feels forced or difficult to be positive about your experience, taking the high road has a way of lifting your spirits in the long run, making you feel stronger and more in control of the situation, and serving as a great example to others of how positive and gracious you can be.

When Valerie's husband Wally retired from his teaching position, they decided to move to Palm Beach, FL, where Valerie continued to pursue public speaking, published a second book, and, on her seventy-second birthday, was signed to a new modeling contract with Wilhelmina Models, one of the world's top agencies. She continues to speak regularly all over the country and most recently was hired as executive editor of a new lifestyle magazine focusing on the baby boomer market called Fabulously Fifty Plus.

Valerie's second act appears to have no end in sight.

Part III.

REINVENTION: A PRACTICAL METHODOLOGY

THE BOOMER REINVENTION METHODOLOGY, which I'll outline for you in the next five chapters, emerged from the lessons I have learned and the steps I have taken in recovering from my own career setbacks over the years. It's a common-sense plan that you can follow regardless of your specific circumstances or situation. The key goal of the system is to help you think more expansively about yourself, using your imagination and your inner-knowing to figure out what your next steps should be in accessing the next stage of your career.

In my own career and in my coaching practice, I have found the Boomer Reinvention sequence of five steps and twenty-three underlying strategies to be a viable blueprint for career reinvention. However, nothing is carved in stone. You should feel free to use what you find most useful and relevant. Nor should you feel as if the steps must be followed in order. Use the book as a baseline, but modify the system in whatever ways suit you best.

Here is the summary of the five steps:

1. **Reframing** deals with the various beliefs and attitudes that you have built up over the years about who you are, what you can do, and how the world works. You need to reexamine and reevaluate these beliefs and attitudes, and change or update them in order to see new and different opportunities that may be right there in front of you.

2. **Listening** builds on the Reframing step by encouraging you to be on the receiving end of information of all types and from all sources. In addition to providing exercises that will stimulate you to think and feel differently about yourself and your environment, Listening sets out a process of inviting feedback from friends and colleagues. This process can give you a different perspective on who you are and what you've done. Constructive feedback is essential in developing an accurate picture of how you have been perceived and how your work has had an impact on others—both positive and negative—which will help you to target issues that need to be resolved and bridges that need to be mended.

3. **Accepting** is the reconciliation process you can use to finally clear outstanding past misinterpretations, judgments, and unresolved issues

identified in the Reframing and Listening steps. By putting the past behind, you, you can move forward into the reinvention process with a clear head and an emotionally reenergized focus.

4. **Expressing** is about planning your reinvention. This is the most reflective and uplifting step in the process, where I encourage you to use a number of behavioral and visioning techniques to identify the possible reinventions that will work for you. You'll find that reinvention does not have to be a dramatic, overwhelming shift to something completely new. The kind of fresh attitudes and directions that you can learn in this process can transform your existing job and career just as much as it can lead to a new one.

5. **Connecting** is the process of taking everything you have learned through the first four steps and bringing it successfully out into the world. As we'll explore, there are many new ways of approaching your career in the digital age. Taking your cues from the information covered in the first two chapters, Connecting covers ways to better implement the reinvention plan you have created in the Expressing step.

I don't subscribe to the notion that a successful career is about "finding your bliss." This is a lovely, romantic idea that is not really grounded in reality. If it were indeed the case, then every TV talent show contestant would be a superstar. I prefer an idea expressed by the venture capitalist Ben Horowitz in a recent commencement address: follow your usefulness.

Usefulness captures what you can do well as well as where and how you can apply it. Your talent, your skill, your experience, your uniqueness—all have the potential to work together to fulfill a need. As you are doing your research, questioning your assumptions about yourself, using the Boomer Reinvention steps and strategies, and otherwise engaging with your universe and your reinvention, remember to make it useful. If you follow this principle, there will always be a demand for what you have to offer.

All of the worksheets and graphics featured in this Part III are available on the book's website: http://boomerreinvention.com.

Or scan this QR code from your phone:

Chapter 10.

REFRAMING:
EVERYTHING IS POSSIBLE

WE BOOMERS ARE NOT THE SAME people we were in our twenties. Let's stop defining ourselves in the same terms and by the same criteria that we created at that earlier time. We've lived through a lot since then and are continuing to acquire new experiences. Isn't it time to reframe our beliefs about who we are and what we can do and to leverage the wisdom and experience we've acquired?

What I am describing as Reframing is a conscious process of choosing to redefine our beliefs and attitudes and to create a new, better, more effective, more efficient, and more harmonious process of planning and pursuing our career. As Charles Kettering, the first head of research and development at General Motors, said many decades ago: "If you've always done it that way, it is probably wrong."

We all carry judgments and beliefs that we don't question but that may be outdated. We don't even recognize them as judgments. We just think of them as normal. Yet we may be using them to put limitations on what we can do and how we could change.

Even worse, we are so used to these ideas and have been operating with them for so long that we don't even realize that they are holding us back or that there might be another way of looking at our situation. We tend to make knee-jerk assumptions: "Oh, I can't do that." "Ask me to do anything, but not that!" "Oh, that's not me. I don't work that way."

So we are more likely to stay stuck in our comfort zone, in that familiar mode of living that we've been stuck in for years, rather than risk some discomfort and uncertainty in the process of changing our lives around. We may think we want to change our lives, but we're waiting for some external signal or event to make change happen. We don't think of changing our way of thinking or our way of looking at the situation.

It's ironic: we keep looking for a way to change our lives without having to change our lives to do it.

Reframing is the process that calls those outdated realities into question and tries to come up with alternative perceptions that may actually be more accurate and more supportive for us than the old ways we've been holding onto.

Successfully reframing our views and our beliefs frees us to see the world and ourselves in a different light. Unshackled from the beliefs that may be putting limits on our abilities because of fears, not facts, we may now be in a position to entertain new ways of living, new ways of working, and new ways of relating to our family, friends, and colleagues. Reframing is the first step toward liberating ourselves from the confines of our "stinking thinking" and the limiting beliefs of our past.

YOUR ATTITUDE ABOUT THE ISSUE IS THE ISSUE

A big reframe for me occurred at a crisis point in my career, around the turn of the century. When my tech startup finally went belly-up after the dotcom bubble burst in 2001, I found myself back on the street without a job and unsure where to turn. I was feeling discouraged and wondering how my years of hard work had led to this apparent dead end.

In the midst of this uncertainty, I happened to run into an entertainment business colleague whom I hadn't seen in years. As we were catching up, he stopped me in the middle of the conversation and said, "You know, I just have to tell you—I've always admired the way you've handled your career. You championed some really innovative movies, you've worked overseas, and you got into technology very early on. . . ." He continued to acknowledge this seemingly maverick aspect of my career, but I was flabbergasted. Here I was thinking that my career had been a series of struggles and washouts, and here was a guy who saw me as having a varied and dynamic career.

My limiting belief was that my career had been a debacle, and when I compared myself to people who had been more conventionally successful I felt convinced that there was something wrong with me. Because of this belief, I was tempted to dismiss my friend's words as unrealistic and inaccurate. But I stopped myself just long enough to notice a little glimmer of a realization in my consciousness: "What if he's right?"

What he said haunted me after we parted ways. I thought, "Okay, let's play this game. Let's see if I can reframe my career and look at it a different way." I decided to look at my career, with its many twists, turns, and job changes, as an extension of my own natural curiosity, my project-based orientation, and my need to explore new ideas and to conquer new challenges. I realized, for better or worse, that is indeed who I am and what I love to do. I came to accept that I have a short attention span and get bored easily, and that I'm not a good steady-state manager. Yes, I admit it! If you want to design a new program, I'm your guy. If you want to bring a new team together, motivate them behind a vision, evolve that vision into a working plan, and implement that working plan through all the iterations, change-orders, and uncertainties, then let me take charge.

But once I've tied the ribbon around it, hire someone else to run it! That part of the job is just not me.

That single reframe—seeing myself as a career explorer and a serial problem-solver rather than a serial failure—became a small but critical window to regaining my confidence and believing in myself once again. I discovered that the real issue for me was not that there was something wrong with me or my career, but that I was looking at myself and judging myself inaccurately. Through this reframe, I understood that I was not a failure for not finding a steady-state, stable management job. I realized that I was chasing the wrong idea of success, and that success for me was fully committing to a more entrepreneurial approach to my career.

We need to take responsibility for the things we can change and work around the things we can't. And one thing we all have the power to change is our own attitude.

Here are some specific techniques you can practice that will help you begin to engage in reframing your attitudes about yourself, your life, and your career.

FOCUS ON WHAT YOU CAN CHANGE

Successful reframing starts by narrowing your focus to the issues that have the most impact on your day-to-day, and are the ones you can actually change through the reframing process. It doesn't make much sense to me to try to reframe what I call Global issues—politics, institutions, nature, and so on—because these are things we can't change. It's much more effective to focus in on what I call Personal issues—your relationship with yourself, including your physical, mental, emotional, and ethical attitude—and Local issues—issues you have with people you know, including your family, your colleagues, your social circle, and the members of your community.

Sure, Global issues may trigger you. You may get all caught up in politics and social injustice, but don't let that distract you or discourage you from focusing on what you can actually change. Focus instead on the Personal and the Local. Take care of yourself first; then devote time and energy to larger projects from the overflow that remains from your own success.

CHOOSE YOUR WORDS CAREFULLY

At the beginning of my psychology training, I was struck by how our use of language influences and programs our behavior in subtle ways. Basically, we have a choice to frame behavior in either positive or negative terms. We can talk about a result we want or a result we don't want. Our word choices influence our results.

For example, when we are dealing with small children and trying to make sure that they are playing or acting safely, we can unknowingly program them to fail. When we say, "Don't drop the milk," the child is thinking ". . . drop the milk, drop the milk, drop the milk." They're hearing the words we just said and struggling to comply because we've put them into conflict. They know they're not supposed to drop the milk, but their unconscious mind is also tied into their eye-hand coordination, and for a split second, this confusion can cause exactly what neither we nor the child want to have happen, because somewhere inside their mind, they're hearing the directive "drop the milk."

Rather than set up a direction based on a negative outcome, we can reframe our words to create a positive outcome: "Hold onto the milk." It's really as simple as that. The positive outcome is linked to the motor skills pathways, and the message is consistent across all channels. Motivational speakers, particularly practitioners of neuro-linguistic programming (NLP) like Tony Robbins, use this technique to turn our negative patterns around and to create positive visions and outcomes.

UNDERSTAND FEAR AND PUT IT IN ITS PLACE

A very wise teacher of mine once pointed out that fear can be viewed as an acronym for *False Expectations Appearing Real.* Fear is one of those reactions from deep in our primitive brains. To this part of yourself, something that is unknown could be life-threatening, and so your fear heightens your physical responses, raises your adrenaline levels, and prompts you to proceed with extreme caution. Fear is also an anticipation of a future that is just one possibility out of many. If that fear is strong enough, it wipes out any consideration of other possible outcomes.

Fear is a normal part of life. If you understand that your fears may not actually reflect reality, then your fears become somewhat more manageable. Expect that fears will come up regularly over the course of your reinvention experience. Rather than allowing yourself to be controlled by them, you can (and should) reframe them!

FIVE REFRAMING STRATEGIES

To get the reframing process going, I'm going to suggest five strategies that you can do to shift your perspective, which is built on your past, and shift it into your present, so that you can start making unencumbered decisions about your future.

Read through these strategies and download the worksheets from the website. You can do these strategies in any order, and you can always come back to review and update them as you pursue your reinvention. As new ideas pop into your head, and as you get feedback from close friends and advisers in the upcoming Listening step, you may want to review these worksheets to update your reframes and make them more consistent with what you're discovering about yourself and about what you want to do going forward.

These strategies create a set of benchmarks. You can periodically check back with the worksheets and review your evolving beliefs based on your new experiences. This will help you verify that you are still on track and make any necessary updates or mid-course corrections.

STRATEGY #1. ASSESS THE STATUS QUO

We're taught to prefer the status quo. Humans for the most part tend to like stability, and we strive for it. Once we achieve a certain level of stability and comfort, we try to preserve it as a steady state— something we all know as our comfort zone.

We're taught conflicting things about comfort zones. Publicly, we're taught that we should be adventurous and daring and brave and strong, and that comfort zones stand in our way of achieving success. How many times, in how many self-help books or self-help speeches, have you been told to "get out of your comfort zone"? And like all good, progressive humans, who want better lives, more freedom, and more independence, we agree and pledge to get out there, to break out of our self-imposed shackles and make a difference in our lives and in the lives of those around us.

But we all know that the reality is different. What we are privately taught—by our parents, by our teachers, by our bosses, by

our clergy, and by other powerful influencers—is that the comfort zone is where we should live. We should be happy with what
we have; we should accept our lot in life. We should "go along to
get along."

So the first step in Reframing is to question your comfort zone. To
do this, you must assess your status quo. What follows is a checklist
that will help you do this.

BOOMER REINVENTION WORKSHEET #1		
REFRAMING CHECKLIST		
Date:		
Comfort Zone	**Status Quo**	**Reframe/Next Steps**
My Job (current or former)		
My Education/Training		
My Talents		
My Skills		
My Dreams		
My Routine		
My Income		

For each Comfort Zone category, fill in your current thoughts or perceptions of where you are in the Status Quo column. For example:

- My Job: "Stable, but unsure long-term"
- My Education/Training: "Well-prepared"
- My Talents: "Great at mentoring"

Then for each category, decide the changes that you need to make or would like to make in order to pull you beyond your comfort zone and be more proactive. Write these in the Reframe/Next Steps column. For example:

- My Job: "I'm reengaging with my supervisor," or "Pursuing a new direction in the same industry"
- My Dreams: "Spending more time writing my book"
- My Routine: "Commit to twenty minutes of meditation three times per week."

Don't feel obligated to fill in every box. However, it's a valuable exercise if you're willing to give it a try. The point of this exercise is to jog your mind from any fixed ways of thinking about any particular aspect of your current picture.

You should print out several copies of the checklist and experiment with different versions. You might come up with a preliminary set of actions, reframes, and goals that you can start to implement in the weeks to come. Here's what one version of this checklist could look like.

BOOMER REINVENTION WORKSHEET #1

REFRAMING CHECKLIST

Date:

Comfort Zone	Status Quo	Reframe/Next Steps
My Job (current or former)	Very insecure, feeling isolated, could get let go?	Be positive at work. Figure out Plan B
My Education/Training	No change	Do I need new credential? Investigate classes?
My Talents	Connecting people	Where else could I put this to good use (at work or outside)?
My Skills	Communication, writing, also working w numbers	Build different work/biz around skills? Get advice, support?
My Dreams	My own business	Research franchises, Maybe take over existing franchise? What are my criteria?
My Routine	Healthy diet, not much exercise.	Exercise 1+ day/week!
My Income	$75k	$150k. What do I need to do to get there? Quit? New Biz? Side biz? Partner with ?

STRATEGY #2. REFRAME THE PERSONAL AND THE LOCAL

The next step in tackling the Reframing process is to deal with all of the ingrained beliefs you have about how the world works, which are largely drawn from experiences you have had on the Personal and Local levels. These beliefs and experiences have accumulated over time, but that may be outdated. You may discover in reevaluating your beliefs and experiences that they no longer apply. You may discover that you have been holding onto a particular point of view that could be updated. The exercise is as much about evaluating and questioning the status quo as it is about actually migrating your point of view to a new way of thinking. You may, at the end of this process, decide to maintain your current point of view or perception—but now you will know *why*.

Reframing the Personal and the Local is a great way to begin a counter-narrative that chooses and uses different words to redefine your point of view so as to yield more positive results.

BOOMER REINVENTION WORKSHEET #2		
REFRAMING PERSONAL/LOCAL #1		
	Disappointments	Defeats	Obstacles
1			
2			
3			
4			
5			
REFRAMING PERSONAL/LOCAL #2		
	Disappointments > Lessons	Defeats > Opportunities	Obstacles > Insights
1			
2			
3			
4			
5			

List up to five experiences under each column of section #1.

- **Disappointments:** The significant letdowns you've had in your life. This could be where someone disappointed you, you disappointed someone else, or you disappointed yourself. They could relate to a friend, a colleague, an offspring, or a spouse. They could be jobs that you didn't get, a bad choice that your son or daughter made, a business deal that you didn't close, or your inability to stick to a diet or to give up smoking.

- **Defeats:** Significant times or events where you experienced a decisive setback. For example, the time you got fired from a job, got burned in a divorce, had a business or a project fail, or suffered a public or personal humiliation.
- **Obstacles:** Things that seem to keep recurring to block your way in life. Perhaps it's a bad habit or an addiction, a challenging professional relationship that undermines your confidence, a disability of some sort, or something that you feel you are lacking, such as education.

Now reframe each of the elements you wrote down in each of the three columns in section #2.

- **Lessons:** For the Disappointments, ask yourself what you learned from the experience. You may have learned something about yourself, someone else, or the way the world works—for example, maybe you put your faith or trust in someone who didn't deserve it. Understanding the lesson will help you avoid making this mistake in the future.
- **Opportunities:** For the Defeats, ask yourself to define a positive way of assessing the situation. Maybe losing a client or a project forced you to find a new approach that ultimately led to a successful outcome. Maybe a defeat revealed areas in your practice where you could improve.
- **Insights:** For the Obstacles, ask yourself how confronting them gave you more perspective. For example, maybe you had to work harder to get around the negativity or disorganization of your company's leadership. That may have taught you a lot about resilience and your ability to think critically and proactively.

Here's how your exercise might look:

REFRAMING PERSONAL/LOCAL #1		
	Disappointments	**Defeats**	**Obstacles**
1	Losing contract w. long term client.	Getting fired after 10 years.	Supervisor standing in the way of promotion.
2	On business trip during son's graduation.	Seeing colleague leave company and take one of my accounts.	Lack of advanced degree.
3			
4			
5			

REFRAMING PERSONAL/LOCAL #2		
	Disappointments > Lessons	**Defeats > Opportunities**	**Obstacles > Insights**
1	Really look at where I dropped the ball.	Job was confining me. I was always complaining. I was at the wrong company	Double-down on my proven abilities, look elsewhere for work, trust myself!
2	Stop letting the job run me.		Appreciating what I know and have learned.
3			My bad experiences don't define me.
4			
5			

The point of this exercise is to pull back from the broken record of negative thoughts or feelings that date back to earlier experiences and to put the wisdom of time and distance to work for you.

Shifting to this updated perspective may help you to effectively close the book on conflicts and bad feelings that you may have been harboring for years, and may trigger or free up additional, more positive, and helpful thoughts. Removing these old patterns from your mind may allow new ideas and inspirations to come forward—which is just what you need for your reinvention journey.

STRATEGY #3. REFRAME LIMITING ROLES
(You Are More Than Your Résumé)

Building on the reframes at the Personal and Local levels, reframe how you have defined yourself through the roles you have played, both personally and professionally, in your life. This is particularly helpful if you are reentering the workforce after spending time raising a family, or if you have been employed in the same job or role for many years.

Our language and culture conflate who we are with what we do. When you meet someone socially and they ask you what you do, a typical answer might be "I'm VP, Sales for such-and-such corporation," or "I'm a graphic designer," or "I'm a professional (whatever)." Each of these responses defines a person in terms of who he or she is. A more accurate reply would be to focus on what you do, by saying "I work as . . .".

We are each much more than the roles that we take on in our work. Our identities do not have to be completely wrapped up in or defined by our jobs. Even if we love our work and can happily spend every waking moment enjoying it, it doesn't define us. We don't need to pigeonhole ourselves into a specific role. If we need or want to, we should be able to take what we love and enjoy about that role and find another one.

Rather than look at yourself as a job description that maps to a certain level of seniority or a set of tasks, think about yourself in terms of the impact you have, or have had, as a person in that role. Take a step back and think about what you actually do in that role that creates lasting effect and value. The exercise that follows will help you do this.

BOOMER REINVENTION WORKSHEET #3	
REFRAMING ROLES	
Current Role:	**Reframed Role:**
Job Description:	Impact Description:
Current Role:	Reframed Role:
Job Description:	Impact Description:
Current Role:	Reframed Role:
Job Description:	Impact Description:

In this exercise, take your current (or most recent) job, and at least two other current roles or previous jobs. Other roles you've been involved in could be charitable and volunteer work, or pro bono work you've done with community organizations, professional associations, clubs, or political activities. For each job or role, compare the Job Description with what I call the Impact Description—what you are actually achieving through your job role.

To fill in the worksheet, write a one-line thumbnail description for each Job Description (it may be your job title), just as you would put it on your résumé.

Now reframe each of these roles by describing them in more active, results-oriented ways in the Impact Description column. If you are not yet functioning the way you would like to function in this role, you may choose to make this reframed description aspirational; to do this, write down this improved version or vision of the impact you would like to achieve in that role.

Seeing all of these roles laid out in front of you may start you thinking more seriously about whether you're happy with what you're doing, or whether you're ready to upgrade your role. Feel free to play around with the possibilities. You may want to draft different versions of these roles to account for different possible scenarios that you envision, including advancing to what you perceive as the next level in your work and involvements.

Here's an example of what your exercise could look like.

BOOMER REINVENTION WORKSHEET #3	
REFRAMING ROLES	
Current Role: VP Sales	Reframed Role: CMO
Job Description: Responsible for supervising sales team in Western Region + customer relationships	Impact Description: Building a collaborative team around company goals, improving client relations, developing new business lines w. sr. mgmt. colleagues.
Current Role: PTA President	Reframed Role: School Board President
Job Description: Organize/chair quarterly meetings, liaise w. school principal & staff.	Impact Description: Working w. families & school staff & edu professionals to deliver a great education experience for our kids.
Current Role: Volunteer	Reframed Role: Shelter Board Member
Job Description: Spend 8 hours/month volunteering at local animal shelter.	Impact Description: Reaching out to our community to raise awareness of pet care issues, drive education initiatives & reduce unwanted & homeless pets.

Understanding how all of your roles fit together can also be of value. It can help to clarify where you want to go in the future and what kind of work-life balance you want to shoot for. Maybe you're taking on too much responsibility in one role and too little responsibility in another. As you age, you are likely going to feel differently about how you want to spend your time than you did in years past.

For many people it is hard to see where or how their skills are portable to new jobs or new companies—or even new industries. As you reframe your roles, look for aspects, skillsets, and responsibilities that could be applicable in fields other the one you've been working in. You may begin to see how you don't need to be defined by or confined to a particular kind of job in a particular kind of company.

Some of the factors influencing your reframe could be:

- Additional training and professional development that you would like to get
- Travel and international experience that could inform a role you would like to take on
- Nonprofit or service work in a different sector (or in more senior managerial capacities) that could apply to your main career role

All of these life experiences count in reevaluating what you now think you can do, or want to do with your reinvention.

STRATEGY #4. ACT AS-IF

Now that you've got some experience in thinking a bit differently, it's time to try acting a little differently as well.

"Acting as-if" is a behavioral tool to help people step into new ways of behaving. It allows you to try out prospective habits and mindsets that you haven't yet integrated into your life. Some examples:

- You may never have owned a business, but what would it feel like to own one? Even if you're feeling stuck in your job or worried that you're about to be let go, act today as if you have your own business already up, running, and making money. How would that feel? Do you think it might put some spring in your step? To find out, spend one day acting as-if.

- If you are struggling to figure out what kind of business you want to launch, what if you just assume you've figured it out? How would that feel, and what would your day look like? Test it out by spending one week acting as-if.

- If you can't stand your boss or a particular coworker, what would it feel like to find that you are suddenly getting along with them beautifully? What would going into work feel like? Discover the answer by spending a day acting as-if.

- If you're hampered by credit card debt, what would it feel like to have paid it all off and to be free of that burden? What would it allow you to buy, invest in, or explore? What would it feel like to manage your finances as if you were debt-free? Try it by living for one month as-if. (But don't get into any more debt in real life!)

Acting as-if is a powerful way to represent the life that you want and are looking to achieve.

You don't have to fool yourself into thinking that your as-if assumption is real—you know you're conducting an experiment. But stepping into the fantasy lets you experience what it could/would/will be like to achieve that fantasy in real life. This then becomes an incentive for you to accelerate your steps toward changing what you need to change in order to make it really happen.

You may find that, if you walk through your workplace feeling as if you and your nasty coworker are besties, it subtly affects your overall attitude and relationships with your coworkers.

You may discover you only need one day of acting as-if for a strategy to pop into your head about how you can accelerate paying off your loans. Maybe the experience will incentivize you to take a harder look at your expenses and channel just a little bit more toward paying off your balance.

Acting as-if has cascading benefits that you will only be able to access once you've tried it. This practice can uncover new ideas about what you want to do or how you want to do it and thereby accelerate your overall reinvention.

STRATEGY #5. REFRAME YOUR MISSION

We're used to thinking about mission statements as motivational mottos for our companies—inspirational ways of describing the meaning, purpose, goals, and values of an organization. I want to suggest that you apply the same kind of thinking to your personal mission, in work and in life. Based on the exercises you have done to reframe various aspects of your life and career so far, how would a mission statement describe the way you want to see yourself going forward from this point on?

In formulating your mission statement, start by thinking about why you want to reinvent your career. While most people would probably talk about achieving meaning, purpose, and income beyond traditional retirement, you may be motivated by a specific desire to serve others in a particular way or to express a particular talent or skill that has been previously underutilized in your life.

Your mission statement should distinguish the new you from the way you have lived up until now. So reflect on the difference and embody it in the mission statement. Be specific about the career focus that you are looking for, and include the kind of work-life balance you are trying to achieve. If any of these elements changes down the road, you can always revise the mission statement.

Your mission statement should inspire you to keep pursuing your reinvention journey despite obstacles and setbacks. You will have some challenging days ahead as you continue to clear material from the past and work at planning out your future career. You're going to want to be able to read your mission statement on those days and reconnect to your values and to the validity of your mission. If the mission statement starts to lose its motivational effect, then you need to go back and revise and update it to reflect what is now energizing you.

Don't feel as if you have to capture your mission in one sitting. Keep the draft handy and work on it whenever you feel motivated or an "Aha!" moment strikes

Share your mission statement with trusted family and friends to see how it resonates with them. Seek feedback on making it more specific, more reflective of your mission, and more inclusive. You want to make sure that it covers and encapsulates all of your top priorities.

Here are a couple of examples of possible mission statements:

"I am continuing to earn income and achieve true balance in my life by launching my home-based business as a virtual assistant in the financial services sector, putting my decades of organizational and managerial experience as a broker to work in a new way for clients all over the world."

"My franchise retail business leverages my decades of corporate marketing expertise, creating a successful stream of revenue and an inviting experience for my customers, and enabling me to build a small team of loyal employees who reflect my values and share my goals for the business."

THEN AND NOW: REFRAMING "EXTRA CREDIT"

You've now completed the five strategies that make up the Reframing step of the Boomer Reinvention methodology. But if you feel motivated to do some extra credit work, here is an additional exercise you can do to deepen the Reframing experience and perhaps gain powerful additional insight. I call it Then and Now.

Start by taking some time to think back to where you were ten or fifteen years ago. Look at photos or other remembrances from that earlier time that you haven't looked at in a while. If you have a journal, notebook, or calendar from that time period, look through it to jog your memory.

Now write a few paragraphs or a page that summarizes the person you were back then, including the work that you were doing and the working relationships that you had. Describe your role, your day-today routine, the people you got along with, and the people who drove you nuts. Discuss or list your accomplishments and things that you were proud of at work, as well as things that didn't go so well—perhaps the time you lost a big client, got fired, or weathered a company merger.

Whatever happened back then, it will likely surprise you to look at it from today's perspective. As you delve into your memories, you will likely see things from a new perspective—the wisdom of hindsight.

Write another page or a few paragraphs drawing the distinctions between where you were then and where you are now. Take note of the lessons you've learned and the perspective you've developed. Particularly look for any indicators that show a certain direction or evolution. You may note that there are certain things that used to really preoccupy or bug you, but that you've let go of those concerns. Perhaps you've developed a real interest in or enthusiasm for something that was never on your radar back then.

Realizing that you have developed this kind of growth and evolution over time makes you more aware of how fluid your life really is. That can also give you some indications and ideas about where you might want to concentrate your reinvention focus going forward.

A FINAL WORD ABOUT REFRAMING

Having worked through the Reframing step doesn't mean that you have to know the solution to your problem or what your reinvented career is going to look like. There's plenty of room ahead to figure that out. Just acknowledging that some of your old ways of thinking about things no longer work puts you ahead of the curve. Just seeing that the old way is only one of many possible options rather than a universal and eternal truth gives you a major head start in reimagining who you are . . . and making the new you a reality.

Chapter 11.

LISTENING:
INFORMATION IS POWER

YOUR REINVENTION REQUIRES MORE than just your desire to change your career around. Dreams are great, but unless you have a well-conceived plan to turn them into reality, they will remain just dreams. Listening is the step in the Boomer Reinvention methodology where you compile a good chunk of the information necessary to formulate that plan.

Gathering information about ourselves and our life plans isn't as simple a matter as you might think. We humans are great at playing tricks on ourselves. We defend ourselves in conversation with others, particularly if the subject matter is sensitive and we feel vulnerable. We listen in order to agree or disagree, not to absorb the information or the intent of what the other person is saying. We prepare ourselves with prepackaged responses to information that we don't like—anything that threatens our sense of ourselves or questions our core beliefs.

The result is that in most of our conversations, we are half listening and half defending ourselves. This is true whether we're discussing personal or business matters and whether we're talking with a family member, our spouse, a friend, a supervisor, a colleague—or especially a potential employer or client. It's a big problem because without accurate feedback from the world around us, we're likely to make serious misjudgments that will threaten the success of our re-invention plans.

Leadership scholar John Gardner once said, "Pity the leader caught between unloving critics and uncritical lovers." It's painful when your critics are beating you up unfairly. But it's just as serious a problem when your friends aren't being honest with you about what you could be doing to change or improve.

The Listening step is about finding the middle ground between those two extremes. Listening involves systematically opening up to receive all kinds of ideas that could spark and sustain your reinvention. You're going to want to talk to a lot of people, read a lot, expose yourself to many different ideas and perspectives, and then organize all of your findings so that you can make sense of them.

The goal is to help you get a clearer idea of where you should be focusing your reinvention efforts. As in any important life decision, you want to be able to balance your internal drives and your instincts with a certain amount of objectivity. You also want to be able to move beyond any complacency or false certainty about who you are and what you can or should do.

SELF-ADMINISTER SOME TOUGH LOVE

Stephen Covey's landmark book *The Seven Habits of Highly Effective People* proposes as habit number five, "Seek first to understand, then to be understood." Among other things, Covey is saying that the smart strategic move is to stop trying to be so smart by coming up with the answer. Sit back, listen to the other person, fully consider what they're saying, and then decide how you're going to respond.

Doing this takes discipline. As we get older, we may feel as if we've seen it all and heard it all. As a result, we may think we're listening when we are actually assuming that we know what the other person or the article or book we're reading is saying. We run everything through an internal filter, deciding what is valid and what is invalid without really examining it closely. We choose to hear what we think is relevant and dismiss what we think is irrelevant. In conversation, we also put a premium on getting our points across—on being heard rather than on really understanding and absorbing what we hear. Don't fall into that trap. This kind of mental arrogance actually closes you off and will prevent you from learning what you need to know for a successful reinvention.

Here are four strategies I recommend for the Listening step of your reinvention process. They will help you to slow down, take a closer look at your decision, and incorporate the insights of others in a really well-developed and practical plan.

STRATEGY #6. PERFORM SOME BASIC RESEARCH

Any new project you embark upon requires information. And any time you are gathering a significant amount of new information, you'll need a system or infrastructure to collect and organize your findings. If you set up such a system early in the reinvention process, you'll be able to adapt it and use it to support everything you'll be doing from this point forward, across all of the remaining steps of the Boomer Reinvention methodology.

I find setting up a system at the start of a project energizing and reaffirming. It reinforces your commitment to yourself that you are really going to do this. There are many possible information systems you can use for your reinvention process, and you may have organized your life or your business using such a system in the past. It can be based on a series of notebooks, loose-leaf binders, file folders, or an accordion file.

For many people in our untethered and mobile world, electronic, cloud-based information organizers have replaced physical systems, and I would wholeheartedly recommend that if you have not yet made the switch to a cloud-based note-taking system, you take this opportunity to migrate to one. It will let you easily compile and review information. There are many systems available, but two of the most full-featured and ubiquitous are Evernote and Microsoft's One-Note. Find an interesting article while browsing the news over coffee? Clip it to your system, whether you're on your laptop or your phone, whether you're at home, at the office, or anywhere you can get reception. You can even use the speech-to-text feature to dictate a note directly into the app. Set up folders or notebooks to match the categories you want to use—for example, "jobs," "new business," "places to live," "things to learn," and so on.

Sources for basic research will fall into a number of categories for you, including information that you'll be able to gather from publications in print and on the Web. Since this step is early in the reinvention process, I would encourage you to create a research and discovery schedule in which you assign a certain number of minutes or hours each week to track down and collect interesting information that could pertain to your reinvention. For example, you might jot down a few professional areas that you're considering or that you've always wanted to learn more about, such as franchises, travel, or graphic design. Maybe you've had a bit of experience in one of these areas, or maybe all of them are virgin territory. Take an hour a day during the week, or a block of time on the weekend, to start searching around in these fields online and learn what you can about them.

As with everything online, you'll find a wealth of information, newsletters to subscribe to, offers of free training or information sessions, and connections to other people who are also interested in the same field. Go ahead and inundate yourself with information. You can quickly unsubscribe to sources that don't end up providing you with valuable stuff. But I feel it's better to overload on knowledge at the beginning, both to get a quick sense of everything that's out there and to get into the habit of collecting and processing a large amount of relevant information. You'll likely be amazed at how energized you feel about this after just a few weeks of immersing yourself in new knowledge about the opportunities available to you.

STRATEGY #7. SOLICIT FEEDBACK

Receiving input from people you know and who know you well is going to be extremely valuable to you as you formulate your reinvention plan. And rather than going for cheerleading sessions (the "uncritical lovers" again), the deeper cut is to solicit constructive feedback that is challenging and eye opening. In this strategy, you will be setting up a series of one-hour conversations (or longer if needed) to receive this valuable feedback.

Listening to honest and constructive feedback can be hard to do. It may reveal things that you are not aware of; it may force you to reexamine cues and clues you have been misinterpreting. This can rock your world. It may expose the stuff you may not want to hear about yourself: the weaknesses you're ashamed of and try to gloss over, the mistakes you've made, the times you've let other people down. But all of these things are part of who you are — or, more accurately, of who you have been—and listening to accurate constructive feedback (more "tough love") can help you clear the past, take responsibility for your actions, and move forward.

You have spent decades in making a living and learning about business and about life and about people. You have left a trail of breadcrumbs behind you that extends back through some very significant, career shaping, and life-shaping incidents and milestones. Soliciting feedback lets you tap into your journey from the past to the present and bring those significant turning points to light. When you reengage with these memories through conversations with people you value, respect, and trust, significant issues are bound to come up, both good and bad. Reexamining these issues will give you some perspective on who you are, what you have accomplished, and where you may have been most effective as well as when you have gone off-track. It will give you a deeper sense of your strengths and weaknesses and reveal perhaps surprising details about how you work most (or least) effectively, what you like working on, and how you have dealt with people. Finally, and most significantly, it will give you clues about what you can do to shape and focus your reinvention, including the right kinds of business ideas, the kinds of businesses you could start, and the kinds of business environments where you would flourish—among other ideas. Being ready and willing to hear this kind of feedback could trigger a real epiphany for you.

Soliciting feedback entails some important procedural and logistical steps, which are outlined below. Don't shortcut the process.

LIST THE PEOPLE WHOSE FEEDBACK YOU WANT

Make a list of between three and ten people with whom you feel comfortable enough to have a serious conversation about your life and career. This can include family, friends and colleagues—anyone who is willing to risk upsetting you a bit by telling you things that you might have a hard time hearing, as true and constructive as they might be.

Of course, you don't want to talk to people who are going to take your invitation as a license to dump all of their pent-up resentments on top of you. You want to choose people who have the compassion and the maturity to truly be of service to you and support you! So choosing the people whose feedback you'll solicit can be a delicate balancing act.

Don't include people who really do not know you well. You may get seduced or deluded into believing that someone new and different in your life is in a position to give you a fresh perspective. If you are tempted to seek out feedback from someone in this category, put them at the end of the list, and get their feedback only after you have heard from everyone else.

You want to include your best friends from school, from work, from your clubs and organizations. They may have a hard time giving you constructive feedback because they are afraid that it will ruin your relationship ("uncritical lovers" again). Try to convince them that if they are true friends, they will be willing to explore the difficult elements from your past that they may have avoided talking to you about. This could this be an opportunity to clear something that is standing in the way of your career reinvention, and it might also be something that clears and deepens your existing friendship.

If you're feeling a bit more adventurous and willing to take a bit of a risk, you might also want to invite one or two people with whom you don't feel very comfortable—the colleague at work who always seemed to criticize your projects or the former boss who let you go. If these are people who, despite your past dealings, have integrity and who you actually respect, you might be surprised at their response to your request. I would bet that their feedback will be among the most valuable that you receive.

People who are not familiar with the value of giving and receiving feedback may be hesitant to engage with you in this process. Don't push it. If someone you invite is not comfortable, move on to other people who will be more willing to work with you.

DRAFT AGENDAS

For each conversation, come up with an agenda—an outline and a set of goals or intentions, together with the questions you want to ask that person.

This gives you the chance to really think about the information and feedback you're looking for in each case. It might involve some very specific questions—things like the resolutions of old hurts or disagreements, learning whether or not a particular perception of yourself is valid or invalid, or going over a series of career options that you've thought of and asking the other person to weigh in. There may be many potential questions that require careful targeting and winnowing. Give yourself a few days or even a week to get this in order. Don't rush through it. Work on the list in your note-taking app and tag each question with the people who you think would be appropriate to answer it, or start with a list of the people you're going to talk to and write appropriate questions for each one.

Sometimes the most valuable feedback and perceptions come from an unexpected source. You will also probably want to get multiple perspectives on the same questions, so be imaginative and wide-ranging as you craft your agendas.

Some ideas for questions include:

- What mistakes did I make?
- What were my best/worst qualities as a colleague?
- What unresolved issues do we have between us, or do I still have hanging with others?

- What are my strengths/weaknesses at work? As a person/ parent/leader/colleague?
- What do you see as my greatest successes and failures?
- What is something that I don't know that I don't know?
- Where do you see me heading in my career, and what suggestions do you have?

More questions will probably occur to you as the meeting approaches. Keep track of these and add them to your note-taking app. Don't think that you will remember the question or the issue in the interview if you haven't written it down. You won't! Treat a reinvention feedback interview as if you are meeting with an important client or going on a job interview. Plan ahead to ensure you make the most of the opportunity.

SCHEDULE THE CONVERSATIONS

Don't conduct your feedback conversation on the spur of the moment. Don't just turn to someone at a barbeque and ask them, "Say, would you mind stepping over to a corner for five minutes to give me some feedback on my career?" Plan it out. Respect their time and your time. This means:

- No going to a party with the intention to corner five people to ask them your set of questions
- No turning to a friend at work and asking them if they've got a few minutes to help out with your reinvention
- No springing questions on your spouse/partner, best friend, trusted relative, ex-colleague, or whoever at breakfast, brunch, lunch, drinks, dinner, or at a bar, and expecting to just dive deeply into a meaningful conversation

Set a separate appointment to meet them, or talk on the phone or online (via Skype or Hangouts) on a day and time that works best for both of you. You don't want them to be merely squeezing this into their calendar just to do you a favor. You might also send them an advance email with your top questions so that they can prepare as well.

Give yourself plenty of time in case you go longer than expected. An hour is a good block of time: not so short so that you'll have to stop just as you're getting to some good stuff, but not too long, either. You don't want to feel (or have the other person feel) as though the conversation is becoming tedious. Leave yourself about thirty minutes' buffer time to prepare for conversation beforehand and another thirty minutes to reflect and make notes afterward.

CHOOSE THE RIGHT VENUES

For each conversation, pick a location that will help you to avoid distractions. You may want to pick a neutral place, neither home nor office, where you will both feel free to open up with no external pressure or distractions. If you're going out to a restaurant, for example, you want to be in a place where you won't be bothered by loud music or noisy conversations. Go someplace that is special, but not distracting—maybe during off hours. A slightly special setting will send the right signal that this is an important meeting. This will cause the other person to take it more seriously, to think a bit harder about what they say, and to provide greater value to you in the process.

FOCUS THE CONVERSATION

As you start your meeting, pay attention to the other person's state of mind. Listen to what they say; notice their tone of voice and their body language. Your goal is to help them relax and feel comfortable with you. Think about what else they may have going on in their lives right now that could be distracting or preoccupying them. A little encouragement and acknowledgment will go a long way toward helping them focus on the subject at hand.

As you begin asking questions, remember to stay focused, neutral, and receptive. Like a good newspaper reporter or television interview-

er, you are there to get the facts and to be objective. If you disagree
or get emotionally triggered by something they say, make a note to
yourself or ask them to explain more, but try not to react visibly. Your
goal is to get them to keep talking and to explore what they're saying in depth, not to argue with them or explain yourself. This is not
about whether one of you is "right" or "wrong." Remember that they
will likely be feeling awkward and tentative sharing this material with
you, and your role is to reassure and encourage them that it's okay to
talk about all this. You are there to learn, not to judge or to react.

I would not recommend using a tape recorder or smartphone to
record the conversation. Knowing that they're being recorded will
likely inhibit your contacts from being completely candid with you.
Take good written notes instead.

EVALUATE WHAT YOU'VE LEARNED

Take time after the conversation to capture what you heard and
reflect on it. During the suggested thirty-minute buffer period immediately following the conversation, jot down the highlights of the conversation, including

- what you learned,
- what was confirmed for you,
- what surprised you,
- what was similar to the feedback from others,
- what was different from the feedback from others,
- what specific advice they gave you, and
- what lessons you gleaned.

If further details occur to you during the days that follow, go back
to your notes and expand them. Pay particular attention to the emotional triggers that you experienced during the conversation. Those
are likely the most important areas for you to think about. They probably reflect areas or experiences where you feel vulnerable, ambivalent, angry, or ashamed about something in the past.

After a few feedback sessions, you should start to get a more complete picture of how you have been perceived over the years, including all of the positive aspects of your life and achievements as well as the challenges you have experienced. Don't use these conversations as an excuse to beat yourself up for the bad stuff or to justify yourself because of all the good stuff. Regard everything you learn as more information, more reference points, for your ongoing reinvention process.

To keep track of your conversations and to help you see whether certain patterns emerge across multiple sessions, use the Feedback Takeaways form below.

| BOOMER REINVENTION WORKSHEET #4 | | | | | |
| FEEDBACK TAKEAWAYS | | | | | |
Person	Successes	Failures	Lessons	Advice	Surprises

Use the Surprises column to list anything unexpected, including things the other person said and how you felt about what they said. You might also include in this column memories or ideas that popped into your head unexpectedly.

Here's an example of a filled-in form:

| BOOMER REINVENTION WORKSHEET #4 | | | | | |
| FEEDBACK TAKEAWAYS | | | | | |
Person	Successes	Failures	Lessons	Advice	Surprises
Jim friend	I'm responsible, engaged w. the world	Can be flakey, self-involved (?)	Need to listen more.	I should work w. people in some way.	Thinks I'm funny.
Ellen – colleague	I'm a good co-worker, understanding person.	I get judgmental, sometimes aloof.	Listen. Connect to the understanding part of me.	Find something purposeful (duh)	(nothing really)

| Fred – ex boss | Responsi-ble – I take ownership. | I don't always collaborate well (true?) | Believe more in myself. | Partner more – seek them out even when not asked to▯ | Really valued my contribu-tions in that job! |
| Susan – aunt | Inquisitive – always finished tasks | Often removed, distant as a kid | Be bolder. | Define my dream and go for it. | (nothing) |

Use this form as a reference to recall the significant highlights of your feedback conversations. The information it contains will be useful as you continue to map out the possibilities for your reinvention process.

SEVEN CONVERSATIONAL TIPS

Here is a list of tips you can use to make your feedback conversations more effective and more productive. These can help clear up misunderstandings and promote effective communication.

1.   Perception checking is a way of making sure that you hear what you think you're hearing. A simple "What I hear you saying is . . ." can go a long way toward clearing up a point and bringing you closer with the other person. It also makes the other person feel validated and acknowledged. Perception checking applies to feelings as well as to ideas. You may pick up on the other person's emotions and want to make sure that you are interpreting them correctly. So you might offer something like, "Am I understanding that you're upset about this?" They may actually be feeling something different. Using perception checking to make sure that you're on the same page with them emotionally can prevent a misunderstanding.

2.   Open-ended questions are the best way to stay neutral with the other person while interacting in a way that moves the conversation along.   Rather than saying, "What you're describing sounds terrible," try saying, "How did you feel about that situation?" It is a way of respecting them in the conversation and not making assumptions about their intent.

3.   Prizing is unadulterated positive regard for the other person. It is a way of encouraging the other person to feel comfortable and to feel acknowledged. We're asking them to be candid and revealing so it will be helpful if we show our appreciation. Encourage them with intermittent statements like, "I really want to hear what you have to say," or, "I appreciate where you are coming from," or, "Your perspective on this is really valuable."

4. "I" statements encourage communication, whereas "you" statements often sound accusatory. Using "I" statements prevents us from making value judgments that could put the other person on the defensive. Rather than say, "You always got the better assignments at work," you could say, "I felt disappointed when you were given what I thought were better assignments." Rather than sounding like an attack, the statement takes personal responsibility and sounds like an expression of openness and vulnerability.

5. Stay neutral. Even if you feel yourself getting triggered by something the other person is saying. Try to let it wash over you and keep listening. Getting defensive and reactive isn't going to be helpful or productive. It doesn't matter in the moment whether they're right or wrong; they're just sharing information from their point of view. You'll assess the conversation later and decide whether what they shared was valuable of not, whether it was true for you or not, and what you should or shouldn't do about it.

6. Maintain open body language. It's important. It sends subtle signals to the other person and prompts them to either stay engaged or to withdraw from the conversation. Pay attention to how you are sitting during the conversation. If you feel yourself start to sit back, cross your arms, or cross your legs, you may be feeling defensive and beginning to withdraw. Try to lean back in, open up your arms and legs, and move into a more receptive posture. Similarly, if you're starting to fidget or tap your foot, take a breath and let go of the anxiety. These conversations can bring up uncomfortable feelings, so staying open is important.

7.   Accept silence. Silence can be revealing, and it can also be a bonding moment. It can be an opportunity for you and your contact to reflect on your conversation and take stock of what you are learning or realizing about the past or about your relationship. A silence may prompt one of you to say something you have been waiting to say since the beginning of the conversation but haven't had the chance to say yet. Don't waste a good silence by driving over it. It may just be the change that the conversation needs to deepen to a new level or shift to an important topic.

STRATEGY #8. ADOPT NEW WAYS OF LISTENING

Listening is about receiving information in every way, not just through your ears. That includes learning visually through observation and incorporating all the information and feedback you can get about your interactions with yourself and others in a business and a personal context. Allowing for other ways of perceiving and receiving information broadens your overall perspective and can unlock new levels of understanding.

We like to talk about our "bucket list" as if it is something improbable and humorous and somewhere down the road. Secretly, I think many of us never expect to check off very many of the items on that list, and we chalk it up to the way life works and to the fact that the bucket list may be mostly a fantasy. For our reinvention, I think we have to explore what we are not used to exploring.

LEVERAGE YOUR SLEEP STATE

One intriguing way to listen to what is going on inside you is by researching your own dreams. The psychology of dreams is certainly a layered, complex, and controversial arena. I'm not suggesting or proposing a particular point of view about the absolute meaning of dreams, or how they definitively relate to career reinvention. However, for many people, dreams are a reflection of their state of mind and a place where issues of our current lives take on an imaginative or even scary dimension.

Make a note of your dreams (if you remember them). Jot down the feelings you had in the dream, and then as you woke up and remembered it. For me, the feelings around the dream are sometimes more important than the substance or the story of the dream itself.

Your dreams may or may not provide anything valuable. However, in my own experience, I have often awakened from a very vivid dream with a valuable piece of insight.

One way to get value out of your dreams is to set a *bedtime intention*. This is essentially an instruction from your conscious self to your unconscious self to tap into whatever field of knowing that occurs while you're asleep and to route it through to your waking state as you wake up. Before you go to bed, just before you turn out the light, state this intention as a request for assistance. I always ask that this be "for my highest good," as a way of avoiding any negativity or unintended conflicts. Here's an example of what my bedtime intention might look like:

For my highest good, I ask for assistance in clarifying a career path that will be fulfilling, purposeful, and financially rewarding, taking into account my personality, my lifestyle, and my values.

I invite you to customize it to suit the question(s) that you would like answered or supported. You could ask for something more specific:

For my highest good, I ask for clarity in finding a name for my new company—one that reflects the products I will be offering as well as the care and integrity that will go into them.

If you try setting a bedtime intention, you may find that your unconscious mind sends one or more messages to your conscious mind, either in the form of a dream or an actual verbal message.

When I do get a message through this process, it rarely comes in above the level of a mental whisper. Usually, as I'm coming around early in the morning, in the minutes before I actually wake up, an idea will pop up or I'll see things or hear things that are not quite dreams and not quite from the waking world either. Your mileage may vary—I share my experience simply as a data point.

If this process intrigues you, keep trying it and see what kind of re-sults you get. I know people who swear by the practice and are very disci-plined about setting their bedtime intentions.

EXPERIENCING NEW SENSATIONS

As part of the process of shaking up your routine and pro-voking new ideas, you might want to change up some of the familiar ways you do things. Then take the opportunity to learn more about yourself by "listening" to your intellectual, emotion-al, and physical reactions to the new sensations that result. Some examples:

- Try eating meals on different schedules, or swapping meal types for meal times—breakfast for dinner, or dinner for breakfast.
- If you're right-handed, try doing certain things with your left hand, like brushing your teeth or scrambling an egg.
- Watch a TV show that you wouldn't ordinarily watch, particularly one that deals with unfamiliar themes or topics. If you like cop shows, watch a documentary. If you're a news junkie, watch a sitcom.
- If you're a sports fan, go to an opera. If you're a classic rock fan, go to a hip-hop concert.
- Change your commuting route one day per week, even if you have to leave earlier than you usually do to make it to work on time.
- Subscribe to a few magazines or online newsletters that cover subject matter you might not be familiar with, such as new areas of science, psychology, nutrition, or culture. If you really want to challenge yourself, subscribe to a periodical that is 180 degrees away from you politically.
- Go out to dinner or to a bar in a new area of town you've never been to before. And try staying out past 1:00 or 2:00 a.m. to see (or remember) what that's like!

- Cultivate a couple of new friends who are at least ten years younger than you are.

PERFORMING RANDOM ACTS OF KINDNESS

Another way of developing a completely new perspective is engaging in a few random acts of kindness. Some people plan these acts out like a project, making time each week to think up and execute a new random act.

A random act of kindness can be anything from putting money in a stranger's parking meter or offering to help someone take their groceries to their car at the market to offering your seat to someone on a bus (regardless of their age). You can engage in acts of kindness at home by sending flowers to your spouse for no good reason, or maybe taking over a particular task that they are used to doing without making a big deal about it. If your spouse loves making breakfast on the weekend, wake up early and return the favor.

Other ideas for random acts of kindness:

- At work, pick a coworker at random, find out what their favorite treat is, and bring it to them one morning.
- If your kid has a regular chore that they're supposed to do, tell them that you're going to do it this week.
- Call someone on the phone with whom you haven't communicated in a while and just have an enjoyable chat without any agenda.

A few years ago, a friend of mine was in a clothing store and overheard a woman talking with the cashier. It seemed that she was from out of town, didn't know the parking regulations, and had had her car had towed while she was in the shop. She had her wallet and ID with her, but all her valuables were in the car and she had no idea where to go. She was asking to use the phone so she could call the city parking bureau, find out where her car had been towed to, and call a cab to take her there.

On the spur of the moment and trusting her instincts, my friend offered to help out. She called the parking office on her cell phone, got the address of the impound lot, which wasn't too far away, and drove the woman there to retrieve her car.

You never know when you're going to have the opportunity to be of service or to extend yourself just a little bit to help someone out, or even to make their whole day.

What does this have to do with your reinvention? Like the rest of the Listening strategies, random acts of kindness inevitably help you shift your perspective. Devising and executing these random acts will necessarily put you in a different frame of mind from your usual day-to-day, and when you are not engaged in the same old routine, unusual or unexpected ideas may come to light. Listen to these new ideas. They may contain the seeds of a new direction for your life and career.

Coming up with these random acts is a creative process—one that is similar to the process you will use in the Expressing chapter to formulate your reinvention plan. It is also an interpersonal process, one where you connect with others in a positive way—sometimes without even being seen or acknowledged. That sense of connection, and engaging in this practice for the purpose of connecting, can help lay the groundwork for finding a meaningful, purposeful career.

STRATEGY #9. BE OF SERVICE

The notion that interpersonal connection is linked to selflessness and service brings us to this final Listening strategy.

If you've lost a job or a business after many years, you may well feel completely adrift. Even after the requisite amount of time grieving over the loss, there is likely a period of complete blankness, when you have no sense of direction, purpose, or meaning. This is a natural and understandable phenomenon. Where we once had a place to go and people we knew and worked with for many years, we're now stuck at home with just ourselves. Unfortunately, the sense of loss and void can lead to depression and a feeling of low self-worth if it goes unchecked.

For a lot of us, one of the most therapeutic activities we can undertake at a time like this is to be of service to others. I classify this under the Listening step because being of service is a great opportunity to be on the receiving end of new perceptions, new perspectives, and new information.

Taking on a regular service project can be immensely gratifying. It could involve volunteering with a school or a clinic or another social services organization. If you've been moping around following a layoff, or having a hard time focusing and figuring out what your second-act career is going to be, you might want to consider having a place to go to once or twice a month where you don't have to think about any of that. All you have to do is show up and be there for the people who need you and the work that you can do for them. You don't have to run anything. You don't have to make any long-term decisions.

You could also benefit from a one-off service experience—for example, responding to a natural disaster by volunteering with the Red Cross or a local charity. Participating in a single project away from home—in another city, state, or country—can be a great refresher, completely changing your perspective while you lose yourself in the project. When you return, you may find yourself much more motivated, energized, and clearer about what you're going to do about your career.

The irony of service is that once you start doing it, it often begins to feel like the most selfishly rewarding experience imaginable. People who do service work often report that the benefit that they get from doing the work feels much more valuable than the contribution they are making. The experience of gratitude—both in terms of the positive appreciation they receive for doing the work and the gratitude they feel for the opportunity to have made a difference in someone else's life—is extremely powerful.

My experience with service work is that it lets my mind relax, and while I'm not trying to think about what's going on in my life and the problems I've got to solve, new ideas somehow appear. On the service project I've been involved in for the past few years, I spend about a day and a half over a weekend, once a month. When I wake up the morning after the project, I usually feel rested in a special way, as if I've had a kind of spiritual spa day. I feel more balanced, more grounded, and ready to get back into my agenda and move forward.

LOOKING AHEAD

The takeaways from the Listening step of the Boomer Reinvention methodology will lead you directly into the Accepting step. There will probably be a number of memories, incidents, people, and related situations that surface in the feedback sessions and through the other strategies that are going to be useful to you. There may be incidents, experiences, and interactions that you either forgot entirely or filed away thinking you understood them completely. Now they can resurface in a completely different light from the way you remembered them.

The Listening step may also have brought back or brought up unresolved issues. You may find that actions you took or situations you were involved with are still lingering and incomplete. Unresolved issues from the past are energy blocks standing in the way of us moving forward as renewed people with a clean slate. Now is your opportunity to set these things right, to reach out to the people involved and clear the air—exactly what we'll cover in the Accepting step.

Chapter 12

ACCEPTING:
TIME TO LET GO

THE FIRST TWO STEPS IN THE Boomer Reinvention methodology—Reframing and Listening—have encouraged you to reframe ideas and past situations and to listen to feedback and new information. Now, in the Accepting step, you get to clean out the lingering memories and unresolved material that could be standing in the way of your future. We've all picked up a fair amount of baggage along the way, and it's time to stop lugging it around with us. Accepting is about getting to a place where you can talk about past disappointments and discomforts in your career without any awkwardness and own them as learning and growing experiences.

In this chapter, I'm going to invite you to:

- free yourself from inhibitions you have about past job mistakes, embarrassments, or humiliations,
- move past any sense that you're playing the victim,
- assert and reclaim your individuality,
- adopt a compassionate attitude toward yourself and others, and
- create a written affirmation to sum up your sense of yourself and to lead you into the final two steps in the Boomer Reinvention methodology.

One of the keys to the Accepting step is developing a new and healthier attitude toward failure. Most of us spend our careers trying to figure out how to create success while avoiding failure. But in the best startup cultures and the most creative businesses, failure is revered as the best and only way to ultimately succeed. It is no secret that we learn best from situations that are the most fraught and the most challenging. Failure has an uncanny way of heightening our willingness and ability to understand and accept lessons. Thomas Edison's infamous quote is the perfect reminder: "I have not failed. I've just found ten thousand ways that won't work."

As boomers coming around the bend to the home stretch in our careers, we can reframe our supposed failures as constructive lessons, accept and embrace them as important growth milestones, and most importantly use them as springboards for further achievement.

HERE'S AN EXAMPLE OF THE ACCEPTING PROCESS IN ACTION.

A client of mine—I'll call him Martin—was in a quandary. As a brilliant and successful young lawyer, he had developed an interest in public policy. He developed a thought leadership practice that led to his running a small but influential think tank. Over time, however, he began to tire of what had become a somewhat routine job. Approaching sixty and feeling increasingly antsy, he began looking around for something else to do, but couldn't identify the direction he wanted to take. Martin had briefly partnered in an internet business with some colleagues during the bubble of the 1990s, so he was not unfamiliar with the process of starting a business and being an entrepreneur. Still, he was hesitating. So he came to me for advice.

We worked through a number of the Boomer Reinvention processes to identify what was holding him back. Despite his accomplishments and his entrepreneurial experience, he couldn't shake the feeling that any business he started so late in life was doomed to failure. As a result, he'd become resigned to riding out his current think-tank position until he just couldn't stand it anymore.

During one of our sessions, I asked Martin to talk more about his startup experience from the 1990s. We discovered that this was the source of his hesitation. It turned out that Martin was harboring a certain amount of shame and embarrassment for what he perceived as the failure of that business, and he was afraid of exposing himself again for fear that the same thing would reoccur. If that happened, he believed, the emotional and financial repercussions would be too much to bear.

We kept talking this issue through in subsequent conversations, and Martin began to see that what had happened to his earlier business was not his fault—that he had actually handled the demise of that business with integrity and fairness to his partners and employees. Consequently, despite having lost their money, his investors had remained on good terms with him. This conversation gradually helped Marin start his own self-forgiveness process, leading to the realization that he could again trust himself to start a new business.

Past failures don't reflect who you *are*. They reflect your past behavior—what you did. You can learn lessons from them that can enable you to make better decisions going forward. In fact, at this point in your life, you have likely already made the biggest mistakes you're going to make! The chances are good that you are in a much better position to make smarter, more successful choices in the future.

So why let yourself be limited by the past? It's time to let Accepting work its magic. Here are five strategies that will help.

STRATEGY #10. RECONCILE YOUR RÉSUMÉ

There's a job that I never used to put on my résumé. I really needed a job, and so I took it for all the wrong reasons, despite the fact that it was not a good fit for me. After six months, I got fired—suddenly and unceremoniously. Someone once told me, "God fires you from jobs you're too dumb to quit." That certainly applies to me and this job.

Perhaps knowing it was the wrong job for me made me feel especially bad about it when they fired me. I was angry in part because I had just brought the company an important client they would never have been able to sign without me. That success was enough to make me feel I "deserved" the job, despite the fact that I knew deep inside I wasn't the right person for it. More seriously, I judged myself for taking the ill-fitting job rather than believing in myself enough to wait for something better.

This painful episode proved to be an important turning point in my career. I began a period of freelance work that was difficult and stressful but ultimately led to an exhilarating experience starting a tech company during the '90s dotcom era.

For years I left that job off my résumé because the memory just felt so humiliating. I never wanted to talk about it or think about it again.

Maybe, like me, you have a job, a period of time in your career, or a particular relationship that you would rather leave off your résumé so you can avoid thinking or talking about it. If so, you probably realize that this is a problem. To be well prepared for a job interview, you need to be able to talk about everything on your résumé and explain any time gaps without betraying any sense that there's something hidden away that you don't want to talk about. Savvy HR people and hiring managers know when you're holding something back. And when they sense you are concealing something, it waves a red flag, making them uncomfortable on a gut level and unwilling to trust you. That feeling is often enough to make them choose another candidate for the job.

If there is anything in your past that you cringe at having to talk about it, now is the opportunity to deal with it. Accept what happened, come to terms with the past, reconcile the situation and the person or people involved, and move on. You will feel better about yourself, sleep easier the night before an interview, and be thoroughly present, transparent, and authentic in that interview. Your openness will inspire confidence in you, and admiration for how you have successfully moved on from old challenges and are clearly ready to take on new ones.

To accomplish this, complete the following exercise: create a written role-playing dialogue between yourself and whoever you perceive as the antagonist in your memory of the painful past experience. The antagonist is the person around whom your uncomfortable emotions are centered— definitely the person who fired you, but also perhaps someone who harmed, exploited, or abused you in another way, or someone whom you may have treated unfairly and therefore may feel guilty about.

The Résumé Reconciliation Dialogue involves several steps. It starts with a statement describing the situation or incident, naming the antagonist, and sharing your current feelings about what happened. Next, switch roles: imagine what the antagonist might say to you today in looking back on the incident. For example, it's possible the antagonist might offer an explanation and some context for why they did what they did. Then switch back to yourself and reply to the antagonist, trying to understand their position, being open to their point of view, and being willing to share responsibility for the situation. Switch again and give the antagonist one final opportunity to achieve closure by saying something conciliatory about the incident. Finally, switch back to your own voice, and say something to resolve and close out the incident by acknowledging what you've learned from the experience. Use the worksheet that follows as you work your way through this exercise.

BOOMER REINVENTION WORKSHEET #5	
RÉSUMÉ RECONCILIATION DIALOGUE	
Experience:	
Summary/Antagonist	
My Feelings	
My Story	
Antagonist's Story	
My Reply	
Antagonist's Reply	
My Closure	
Antagonist's Closure	
Additional Thoughts, Takeaways	

If you like, you may use a more free-form format—or no format at all. The key is to capture the back-and-forth dialogue between you and your past antagonist as you imagine it and bring it through to positive resolution. It may feel awkward or embarrassing the first time you try this, but no one is looking over your shoulder. Give yourself permission to use your imagination to bring the hypothetical dialogue to life, even if it makes you feel a little silly.

Here's how I filled in the grid for my own humiliating job experience. The antagonist I'm dialoguing with is Jim, the chief operating officer of the company I worked for briefly.

BOOMER REINVENTION WORKSHEET #5	
RÉSUMÉ RECONCILIATION DIALOGUE	
Experience: Getting fired at APA	
Summary/Antagonist	Took the job, struggled w. it. Out of alignment with the way I work. Often at cross purposes. Uphill battle from early on, despite bringing in business.
My Feelings	Humiliation. Anger. Why didn't they at least give me a warning, or try to work it out, or at least sit down w. me and voice their issues? What a dysfunctional management philosophy (if they had a philosophy.) Angry at myself for taking the job. How could I have been so weak and stupid? Yes, I really needed it, but what if I had held out and reached out to more contacts...?
My Story	Jim: Why did you fire me so abruptly? Why were you so rude to me and so dismissive? Don't you think I was trying to fit in w. the team? I had just brought you a client everyone was falling all over themselves about. WTF?
Antagonist's Story	John, I'm sorry, it just wasn't a good fit. You're a very different kind of guy from the other people at the company. Maybe you were the tipping point between two visions of the company that we were debating. I wanted to go one way, and Roger, who brought you in, wanted to go another way. I won the argument, so you had to go. But face it, you weren't the right guy? Were you happy at the company? I don't think so.
My Reply	You're right, Jim, I wasn't happy. It was a bad match. I just wish it had gone differently.

Antagonist's Reply	Hey, I hear you. Remember that I never said to you that you had done a bad job. I just said, "This is your last day." It was never about you personally. As I said,– you were the wrong guy for us, and we were the wrong place for you.
My Closure	I hear you, Jim,– I think that even though I knew that. I had my blinders on and hoped that it would somehow magically work out. I didn't want to look at the long term picture....
Antagonist's Closure	John, I wish you all the best. You're a good guy, and I know you"ve done some great work since. Sorry, again, for what happened with us.
Additional Thoughts, Takeaways	I feel more resolved about this less triggered. I think the idea that it was just a bad fit takes the sting out of the firing. Makes it easier to think about and acknowledge. And didn't wind up making this kind of mistake ever again.

Obviously, I can't know what's inside Jim's head, then or now. But humanizing him in this dialogue and creating a respectful interaction that reflects much of the reality of what happened between us creates a new, less painful version of the story that I can use to replace the one that has been in my head for twenty years. If it helps me to put this incident behind me and to defuse the emotional trigger surrounding the incident, then I have taken a step toward acceptance. And that, in turn, will help me approach the future with less shame and greater self-confidence.

STRATEGY #11. STOP BEING A VICTIM

When I worked at DreamWorks Animation, I used to take CEO Jeffrey Katzenberg around to some of the colleges and universities in our outreach program to talk to the students. Jeffrey is a refreshingly candid speaker. During one Q&A session in a large auditorium, a student way in the back of the hall called out a question: "Why did you start DreamWorks?" And Jeffrey shot back: "Because I got fired at Disney!"

You could have heard a pin drop. I'm sure every one of those kids was thinking, "Uh-oh, that question struck a nerve." But Jeffrey knew exactly what he was doing. He paused to milk the moment, then continued, "And I have news for you. Getting fired is not fatal." You could hear the collective sound of five hundred kids starting to breathe again as Jeffrey explained how he turned his very public firing from one of the top jobs in Hollywood into a springboard that he, Steven Spielberg, and David Geffen used to launch their studio, DreamWorks.

At the time of his firing, Jeffrey may have been angry and disappointed that Michael Eisner, a man for whom he had worked for almost ten years, had turned on him. But he never for one moment made himself into a victim.

When your career takes a painful turn—whether you are stuck in a job where you don't feel valued, dismissed from a job you love, or caught in the undertow when a company is reorganized or goes bankrupt—playing the victim gets you nowhere. Of course, processing a loss takes time. But the productive course of action is to move as quickly as possible from protesting the loss and blaming yourself or others to turning the situation to your advantage. The question to ask yourself is, "If this is not about my being a victim, then what is it about?"

Try the No More Victims exercise: take a situation where you have felt victimized and develop an objective, strategic approach to making it work in your favor. The worksheet below will walk you through the steps.

BOOMER REINVENTION WORKSHEET #6	
NO MORE VICTIMS	
The Situation	
The Accusation	
Your Victim Position	
A Broader Perspective	
What You Did	
What You Could Have Done	
Lessons, Takeaways	

To see how you might complete this worksheet, let's return to my humiliating firing from the six-month job I never should have taken. Being let go felt like a very personal slap, and I've been sorely tempted to play the victim over it ever since. Here's how I filled in the worksheet as part of my effort to escape the victim role.

BOOMER REINVENTION WORKSHEET #6	
NO MORE VICTIMS	
The Situation	Getting fired from APA
The Accusation	Not really sure: somehow I wasn"t doing a good job, they didn"t like me, ▯ something!
Your Victim Position	I'm angry. I feel worthless, humiliated. Why didn"t they see what a good job I was trying to do? Why didn"t they give me a chance?
A Broader Perspective	It was a lousy fit from the start. I hated it there. The only reason I was there was for the money. It was a dead-end position, with no real upside.
What You Did	I was ashamed and essentially hid, not wanting to confide my humiliation with my friends. I felt embarrassed.
What You Could Have Done	I could have felt relieved and liberated, and by acknowledging it was the wrong fit from the start, could have gotten back into the exploration of a new job much more quickly, and from a much stronger frame of mind.
Lessons, Takeaways	Trust my instincts, and believe in myself. The job was really my mistake from the start and I should have turned it down. I haven't and won't make that mistake again.

RESPECT THE "STACKERS"

People who personify our injuries, the ones we blame for all of our misfortunes, are called "stackers." They're the ones who stack the deck against us—at least in our perception. It is easy to blame the stackers for our misfortune. They are the ones who don't understand us, don't acknowledge us, don't listen to us, criticize us, challenge us, and put us down. The things the stackers say about us wound us deeply, often to the point that we lie awake at night remembering their lies and thinking about the rejoinders we wish we'd been smart enough or brave enough to throw back at them.

But if what the stackers say isn't true, then why does it affect us so much?

The stackers get under our skin because they show us where we are not feeling strong or complete inside ourselves. They're perfect mirrors for the dark and secret ways we already feel about ourselves.

For this reason, stackers can be powerful teachers. Ironically, the stackers may be more helpful in transforming your life and career than all of your well-meaning and supportive friends. What are the lessons that your stackers have to teach you? Look over your résumé and reflect on the stackers you met in your most challenging jobs. Ask yourself:

- How did you feel around the stackers?
- What was the internal vulnerability that they reflected back to you?
- Does their perceived judgment against you reflect a judgment of your own against yourself?
- How are you doing with this vulnerability today? Are you feeling more resolved?
- Would the stackers trigger you today in the same way? If so, you may have some more work to do to resolve that vulnerability.

To turn your relationship with the stackers from a liability into a strength, work to separate the message from the messenger. If you focus on the message rather than the personal feelings surrounding the stackers and the way they trigger you, you will grow stronger and be less vulnerable.

STRATEGY #12. LET YOUR FREAK FLAG FLY

The city of Austin, TX, has a motto: "Keep Austin weird." Austin is the state capital, a university town, and a center of music and the arts in Texas. So it's quite a mix of contrasts—a unique amalgam of different attitudes and philosophies. Keeping Austin weird is about letting Austin be Austin rather than letting conformity to any single quality overwhelm its specialness.

Perhaps now is the time for you to stand up for your own "weirdness." We tend to judge ourselves for the ways in which we are different from others and how we just don't fit the norm. This is particularly true in large organizations, which pressure people to adhere to the company culture and mission. Few people actually fit into those norms, but everyone plays along. Perhaps you have finally outgrown the need for this kind of conformity.

If you feel as if your career and personal lives have turned into an enervating routine that is driving you crazy, it is time to remember who you are, what you stand for, what turns you on, and how you want to live. Particularly if you've been working in the corporate world, it may be time for you to loosen up, lighten up, and trust that you've earned the right to behave a bit more individualistically after years of playing by the rules.

I'm not suggesting that it's time to go all eccentric just because you can. Nor am I talking about the classic reactive midlife crisis, where you begin acting out based on your long-repressed frustrations—buying a flashy sports car and maybe even jettisoning all your old relationships. You can be weird on the inside in your own special way without having to advertise it. The goal of reclaiming your identity is to help make yourself more special and more accessible—both to yourself and to others as a source of inspiration and energy.

Here are some of the ways you might begin reclaiming your identity:

- Think about how you schedule and commit your time. How much of that time is spent feeding your soul? How could you dedicate thirty minutes a day, or an hour or two every weekend, to a new activity that would revive a dormant aspect of yourself?
- Look back at the hobbies, arts, outdoor activities, social engagements, or other practices you once drew pleasure from but have since abandoned. Consider choosing one and jumping back into it.
- Consider dedicating yourself to a new practice of regular reading, concert-going, museum- or gallery-hopping, or other activity that could revive old, cherished ways of thinking and feeling.
- Recall the dreams, fantasies, and wishes you harbored in your teens, twenties, or other earlier periods of your life—dreams like walking the Appalachian Trail, playing guitar in a band, becoming a gourmet chef, or designing your own clothes. Does one of them still attract you? If so, consider taking steps to begin pursuing it, a few hours or days at a time.

You could see reclaiming your identity as evolving into a "Version 2.0" of yourself, having nothing necessarily to do with the career path that you are figuring out. As you spend more time in this 2.0 version and accept it more and more, you'll likely find that those around you begin to attune to your new profile. You'll increasingly be accepted and sought after because of the unique qualities that you are finally embodying, expressing, and sharing. This different behavior could very well inspire unexpected career ideas, or put you in touch with new people willing to help you pursue your career goals.

STRATEGY #13. PRACTICE EMPATHY RATHER THAN SYMPATHY

Empathy is the quality that binds all of your Accepting step strategies. Empathy is acceptance in action—for others and for yourself.

Empathy and sympathy are often confused. Sympathy is feeling sorry for someone who is experiencing pain—it puts the other person at arm's length and objectifies their plight. We sympathize with them as a gesture of outreach, but we don't want to feel what they feel or truly be present with them. We prefer being somewhat distant and superior to them, feeling fortunate that we don't share their troubles.

By contrast, empathy is about placing ourselves in the other person's heart and sharing their experience as our own. Empathy acknowledges the other person for what they're experiencing and for the process they're going through. Whereas sympathy says, "I understand how you feel," empathy says, "I feel how you feel."

Compare the experience of empathy vs. sympathy:

EMPATHY	SYMPATHY
Feeling for the person	Evaluating the person
Closeness	Distance
Acknowledging what's present	Telling them where they should be

Empathy helps you to accept and forgive yourself and others. It is the quality that levels the playing field when it comes to the past. If you can move into empathy for yourself and others (including the stackers) as opposed to viewing people through sympathy and the associated elements of judgment and superiority, it will be easier to get past the old mistakes and embarrassments.

Empathy is a muscle that can be strengthened. As you interact with the world each day, be aware of the judgments that pop into your mind. When you find yourself judging the guy who cuts you off on the freeway, the loud group at the bar, your kid's boyfriend or girlfriend, and, of course, the random commentator on TV, make an effort to shift your focus from your head to your heart and to move from thinking about them to simply accepting them. Experience how the judgments fall away, and how what seemed extremely important a minute ago now seems mostly trivial.

This doesn't mean that you suspend your ability to form opinions or to separate what you believe from what you don't believe. But in that empathetic moment, you just see others purely as fellow human beings, feeling and appreciating where they're coming from and allowing for the possibility that underneath their words and behaviors, they are simply people not too dissimilar from you.

Empathy will sustain you through the Accepting step and into the creative work you will do in the final two Boomer Reinvention steps— Expressing and Connecting. During those two steps, you're going to need to stay strong and believe in yourself in the face of the doubt and confusion that will likely come up. You will need to be patient with yourself, giving yourself space to explore and to play. If you are constantly judging yourself and others, you will be setting yourself up for failure. Staying positive and supporting yourself unconditionally will help you develop and organize your ideas and visions for the future and then take them out into the world. Empathy will help to make this possible.

STRATEGY #14. CREATE YOUR AFFIRMATION

One of this book's guiding principles is the idea that "form follows thought"—the notion that if you consistently align your thinking in a certain direction, positive or negative, you stand a very good chance of creating a matching result. There's nothing mystical or magical about this process. You make hundreds, maybe thousands, of big and little decisions every day, many of them habitual. Setting an intention creates a kind of filter in your mind that helps you make the kinds of choices that will invariably point you down the road to fulfilling your goals. By setting an intention and using behavioral tools to reinforce that intention, you can slowly but surely redirect your entire being toward your goal.

Creating an affirmation is a great way of working the "form follows thought" principle into your life and career. It's an activating statement composed and then recited at regular intervals to shift your attitude and/or behavior. I was first introduced to affirmations over thirty years ago and have used them periodically, especially when I was in the midst of a transition and needed to focus on a particular goal.

There are some ground rules or guidelines that are helpful to follow in the process of composing and using your affirmation:

- An affirmation is a statement of "becoming," not a statement of "being." It uses gerunds (the verb form ending in -ing) to underscore the idea that you are engaged in an ongoing process of making that statement into a reality.
- An affirmation is one sentence. It can be a long sentence with plenty of modifiers, but it works best when its message is contained within a single breath. I'm not sure why this works, but in my experience, breaking an affirmation into more than one sentence dilutes its power.
- An affirmation depends on the positive. Affirmations are not about stopping bad things; they're about starting good things. If you hold a negative set of images in your head or repeat them verbally, even with the intention of stopping them, the negative words and images are still going to dominate the message. Don't defeat your purpose before you start. Compose your affirmation from a completely positive angle, packing it full of positive, uplifting words and images.
- An affirmation is about you. Trying to control or influence what others do through an affirmation is pointless. An affirmation is designed to help you support your own behavior change. It realigns your thought process so that you see possible choices that you didn't see before. By composing and repeating the affirmation, your mind directs itself toward opportunities it sees to fulfill the affirmation.

Here are a few examples of affirmations:

"I am successfully completing and publishing my book on career reinvention for boomers, eloquently expressing my five-step process and making it engaging, appealing, and inspiring to my readers."

"I am working out four days per week, feeling energy, clarity, and a sense of accomplishment, listening to my body and supporting it with healthy nutrition and plenty of rest."

"I am creating my new business, connecting with funders, partners, and customers to support my vision and collaborate with me on a profitable launch."

Starting your affirmations with an "I am" statement really nails the idea that this is about you, focusing on you and what you can control. One approach is to acknowledge what brought you to your present situation as the context for focusing on your future goals:

"I am grateful for all of my past career challenges and accepting them into my life as blessings going forward in my new career."

"I am accepting and honoring all of my previous career experiences, centering in the lessons I have learned and applying them to my continued professional success."

THE ATTITUDE OF GRATITUDE

As you work your way through the Accepting step, you may find yourself experiencing a sense of gratitude. That's a good sign. If you're feeling grateful for everything that has come before, it means that you are completely resolved and there are no lingering bad feelings. The process may never be complete. It's likely you will still be capable of getting triggered now and again. Little barbs of bad memories will pop up from time to time. But if you have been diligent about accepting yourself and your past, you'll find they are easily dismissed. You can laugh them off as exquisitely human little hiccups.

Settling into gratitude is likely to be easier for you as you age. Life is always full of unexpected twists and turns. Appreciating all of those ironies is, for me, the only way to get through it. I don't know anyone for whom life has turned out exactly as they planned or envisioned it.

As you embark on the Expressing step to capture the vision and the plan for your career reinvention, take heart in the wisdom that you bring to the process. You really only need to gently tap into that wisdom to start the flow of ideas and strategies that will lead you to the next stage of your career.

From this point forward, dream big. There is nothing left to hold you back.

Chapter 13

EXPRESSING:
CENTERING, DEEPENING, AND DISCOVERING

THE SCARIEST PART OF MAKING A LIFE change is figuring out what to do next. If you've spent much of your professional life catering to the whims and the agendas of others, you may feel as if you've lost the sense of your *own* agenda. Facing the challenge of figuring out who you really are and what you really want may feel as though you've come to a short stop at the edge of a wide chasm.

My most profound life change—the one that prompted my biggest reinvention and brought me to where I am today—occurred when I hit a major career wall and had no place to go but across that chasm. My reinvention took only a year (2002–2003), and the Expressing step was a crucial component of that reinvention.

Expressing is the umbrella concept for a set of five strategies that you can use to help you realign and consolidate your focus around a career direction that works for you. The Expressing step lets you explore one or more career reinvention ideas and fully consider and develop them before pulling the trigger on a choice. It is not about trying to fit yourself into some job or job category that someone else would like to squeeze you into.

This step gets its name from the idea that it is about giving expression to that inner part of you that already knows exactly what you want to do—first as something that is resonant and useful for yourself, and then as something that is resonant and useful (and creates value!) for others. It's about uncovering your best destiny and finding ways to manifest it.

Think of it as a muscle that has been asleep, and is going to need to start exercising in order to get strong and capable. In that sense, the entire Boomer Reinvention process is like training for a marathon or some other major athletic event where you are building strength and stamina in order to complete it successfully.

PITFALLS TO EXPECT (AND AVOID)

Finding ways to express your deepest self isn't something that will happen overnight. Expect to spend between one and three months on this step of the Boomer Reinvention methodology. Set aside some time at least three days a week to work on the Expressing strategies. After you've been working on them for two weeks and have a sense of how the strategies are going, set an end date for your Expressing process. You can always extend that date if necessary, but a deadline helps motivate you.

Be consistent, persistent, and build a rhythm, incorporating these strategies into your daily lifestyle. Not only will they help you to figure out your career reinvention focus, they will also continue to support you as you pursue and maintain your second-act career.

Start off by giving each of the five strategies a try. Feel free to adapt and modify them to better suit your personality or your situation. My goal is not to force you into a strict methodology, but I encourage you to explore each tool on its own, give it a chance to work by itself, and then see how it works in concert with the other tools.

There is no value in blindly following a particular system. There is always room for improvisation. The real reason you're going to get results is because you're committed and purposeful about your reinvention. From the depth of your commitment, you will find that pretty much any system you want to use will get you to where you want to go. Boomer Reinvention is a set of training wheels. Pretty soon, you're going to be taking off the training wheels and riding your bike on your own.

Not all career reinvention ideas are going to turn out to be right

for you (obviously). Many ideas are like a teenage crush or an infatu-
ation. The idea that initially attracted you may start to fade as you sit
with it over time. Look for the ideas that continue to inspire you and
energize you. These are the ones you want to invest in. If you have
explored them fully and you have acknowledged the inherent risks,
difficulties, and challenges, but are still enthusiastic and feel increasingly certain, then you have likely found a winner.

You may get stuck wondering how to kick off the process, and I
have a suggestion. One of the books I highly recommend to fellow
boomers going through job transitions is Tim Ferriss's *The 4-Hour
Workweek,* a guide to working more efficiently and more effectively in
the digital age. Ferriss upends a number of the work paradigms that
we grew up with and challenges us to be more entrepreneurial and
more freelance, since that is the way the world is going. His goal is
to make you more self-reliant, more conversant with how technology
can serve your goals, and more empowered in your career.

Ferriss asks seven questions that are a great way to start the Expressing step. You might want to print them out and tape them to your
refrigerator or bathroom mirror where you'll be able to ponder them
daily. The questions are:

1. What are you good at?
2. What could you be best at?
3. What makes you happy?
4. What excites you?
5. What makes you feel accomplished and good about yourself?
6. What are you most proud of having accomplished in your life,
    and can you repeat it or further develop it?
7. What do you enjoy sharing or experiencing with other people?

The Expressing step requires a significant commitment of your
time and your energy. It's important to begin it with a clear mind and
an accurate set of expectations. Here are a few misapprehensions that
could undermine your efforts and sabotage your chances for success.
That's why I want to eliminate them from your thinking at the outset.

DON'T ASSUME YOU MUST CHANGE EVERYTHING

People often think that reinvention requires a total change in their lives. That's not necessarily so. The best transition for you may not be a complete makeover—a radical shift to a completely different business or industry, for example. Instead, it may be doubling down on whatever you are already doing and reinventing your career from the inside out. Perhaps it will involve learning new skills, shifting your role, changing your attitude, or taking on new responsibilities. It might also be something more radical, like taking a reduction in salary to better position yourself for a more satisfying or strategic role. Be flexible and open-minded, and let the discoveries you make lead you where you're meant to go—wherever that may be.

BE CAUTIOUS WITH LONG-HELD FANTASIES

Many of us dream of returning in our later years to a career passion that inspired us when we were younger. This can sometimes be a fruitful avenue for reinvention (which is one reason I urged you to explore those former passions in Strategy #12). But trying to transform an old fantasy into a new reality doesn't always turn out well.

A client of mine, a very successful corporate lawyer, spent over twenty years in the legal department of her company, rising to the senior vice president level before she was forced out following a corporate merger. She decided to pursue a career as a public defender, something she had always wanted to do. But after a few months actually working that job, she realized that her ability to help underserved defendants was undermined by the bureaucracy that controlled the system. The moral of the story: it pays to do some serious due diligence before investing time and energy into a career shift that may not meet your expectations.

EXPECT TO EXPERIENCE FEAR AND RESISTANCE

The minute you begin working on the Expressing step, you are likely to run into two obstacles—fear and resistance.

Fear will tell you that you're going to fail at this, prompting your brain to list all the reasons why this process is bullshit and you should forget it. Fear will tell you that the risk of failure is too great and that, whatever your current situation is, it's more secure than wasting time on a pipe dream reinvention. Don't let fear stand in your way. As a wise teacher of mine once told me, you may as well be the winner in your own fantasy. So when fear comes up, focus on the counter-narrative, which is the very real possibility that you could succeed at reinvention and create a fulfilling future for yourself.

Resistance is subtler. It occurs when your brain tells you that you don't really have time for your reinvention, since you first have to take care of the many other important things on your life agenda. The problem is that all of us have never-ending, ever-expanding lists of items on our personal to-do lists: cleaning out the garage, updating our will, organizing our personal finances, upgrading our computer system. . . . Some of these may be genuinely important and necessary. Do those now so they won't distract you from the vital work of reinvention. But many of these seemingly urgent tasks are simply excuses for procrastination. Don't get sucked into worrying about them. Otherwise you will wind up deferring your reinvention forever.

I've compared the Expressing step to standing at the brink of a wide chasm. It's very tempting to turn around and retreat. But in the words of the British statesman David Lloyd George, "Don't be afraid to take a big step if one is indicated. You can't cross a chasm in two small jumps."

STRATEGY #15. KEEP A REINVENTION JOURNAL

Journals are a staple of transformational work. If you have used journals to help you lose weight, to track a business project, or simply to document a particular period in your life, you know the power of the regular practice of just sitting down to write. It is an exquisitely safe and personal process that provides many people with a real sense of sanctuary in their life, creating a mental and emotional space where they can be free to be themselves and to experiment with ideas.

Your Reinvention Journal will serve as a collection vessel to help your mind begin releasing the valuable inspiration that has been locked up inside you for years. Think of it as your connection to a well of information and insight that already knows what your reinvention is going to be and is carefully guiding you there. Rather than a space to detail specific ideas or analyze issues of logistics or strategy, it is an opportunity for your imagination to run wild. Later, you'll take the valuable ideas that pop up and use other tools to turn them into concrete plans, agendas, schedules, and programs.

Starting your Reinvention Journal is easy. First, pick out a notebook you find pleasing to look at, one that you will feel drawn to write in every day. If you're feeling a bit intimidated by the idea of keeping a journal, look for one in a format that feels comfortable and won't overwhelm you—perhaps one with 6x9-inch or 5x8-inch pages and with wide spacing.

The prescription: Write two pages per day, in longhand, with a pen. (You may find that as you get into the process you want to write longer entries, but to get started, two pages is plenty.) Write at the same time every day; make it a ritual. It doesn't matter whether you write in the morning, afternoon, or evening. You can write before you go to bed, when you wake up, after you work out at the gym, before or after lunch. What matters is consistency. If you don't choose and maintain a specific time window to write in, you will tend to fall off track and will start missing days.

The content: Even though this is your Reinvention Journal, you may find yourself, particularly at the beginning, actually writing about everything *but* your reinvention. Just start off with whatever is most present for you at that moment. If you're just waking up, you could write about a dream you had or about your feelings about your schedule for the upcoming day. If you're writing at night or the end of the day, you can write about what happened that day, including wins, losses, ongoing challenges, insights, and so on. You can describe your mood and write about your relationships.

Most journal writers find it hard to write at times. Sometimes the flow isn't there. Sometimes you're in a resistant frame of mind and feeling fed up or shut down. Many of my journal entries over the years have started out with me writing about being angry about having committed to writing the journal in the first place. That's okay. Just write about whatever is coming up in your mind, even if all you can do is repeat it. "I hate writing in this stupid journal" is a perfectly great way to begin an entry. Get your frustration off your chest.

You can even write about the fact that you have nothing to write about. You can write "ham and eggs" over and over, or vent at the journal for being there, complain that you have nothing to say, or curse me for assigning you this dumb journal-writing project.

It's all good. The purpose of this exercise is to begin to access the dormant areas of your mind that have grown used to living in the dark. As you continue to journal ritually each day, those unexpressed areas will slowly start to feed into your writing. Over time, you will be surprised to "hear" what seems to pop into your mind as you write. It could be memories you haven't thought about for a long time. It could be different perspectives or opinions about your work or people you know. It could be creative ideas or solutions for problems or projects you're working on.

After a certain amount of journaling, you will begin to hear things and receive input that relates more and more directly to your reinvention, some of which you can later translate into concrete plans and activities. Just as you start the Reinvention Journal with strings of seemingly random thoughts about your day-to-day life, as that day-to-day life begins to include more and more elements of your emerging reinvention plan, your Reinvention Journal will reflect that activity.

Intriguing and useful patterns of ideas and information will increasingly begin to emerge.

Don't worry about how your Reinvention Journal looks or reads. No one else is going to look at it. You don't have to write evenly or legibly, or with fine literary style. Grammar, spelling, and punctuation do not matter. You don't even have to look at it or read it over once you've written an entry. The purpose of the journal is simple: to bring thoughts into your conscious mind for you to consider.

You'll probably have periods of time—perhaps days or even weeks—where nothing meaningful seems to be coming through in your journal. Just keep writing. If you're blocked, write about your block. There will always be something to write about because you are always in process on something, whether it's positive or negative, productive or distracting. Sooner or later, you will work through the fallow period and begin to channel positive and productive ideas once again.

TAKE THE THIRTY-TWO-DAY CHALLENGE

Once a particular activity is deeply ingrained as a habit, you usually practice it with little effort. It has become a natural activity. You even miss it when circumstances interfere with it on a particular day. So transforming valuable behaviors like exercise and healthy eating into habits is an important challenge.

Behaviorists who have studied this issue have found that the key to making something into a habit is to repeat it at least once daily for a certain number of days. Some experts say twenty-one days, others say thirty days, while others recommend longer periods. In my experience, a month of repetition is a pretty good way to instill most habits. At the very least, a month of daily repetition will give you a sense of accomplishment and the confirmation that you are capable of overcoming distraction and maintaining your focus and discipline when you choose to do so.

So I recommend that you set yourself the goal of maintaining your journal entries every day for thirty-two days—a month with a little extra buffer for good measure. If you do this, you will probably have locked in your journal as a habit, which will then set up a great support structure for everything that you do subsequently to reinvent your career.

Note that if you miss a day, you must set the counter back to zero and start again until you achieve thirty-two uninterrupted days of journal entries. If you are serious about this thirty-two-day challenge, you may need to go through one or two resets before you complete the full cycle. Keep at it! The benefits are worth the effort.

STRATEGY # 16. CREATE A LIVING VISION

In keeping with the idea that form follows thought, if you create a detailed picture in your mind of what you want your life to look like and hold and refine that picture continually, you can begin to actually program that vision to manifest in reality. This is what's known as a Living Vision. It's about tuning into what's really going on inside you—what makes you happy, what gives you meaning and purpose, what aligns with your character and your philosophy. It is not about your will or your mind or your ego. A Living Vision is a way to take everything you know about who you are and apply it to a career choice that truly works for you on every level. It is like an inner business plan you are creating to change your life around.

When I was in the first year of the master's degree program at the University of Santa Monica, I began playing around with the Living Vision process. I wrote a statement of where I wanted to be one year in the future, focusing on the quality of my life and work, not on the specifics of a particular company or particular kind of job. I described the qualities of my hoped-for job, the kinds of people I would be working for, and the people who would be working with me. I described an environment where I felt appreciated and where I could trust others. I described a flat organizational structure where responsibility was more important than hierarchy, where new ideas were encouraged, and where people were given the chance to experiment.

When it came to what my salary was going to be, my Living Vision process hit a bump. I started out by including a salary that I had received in the past, although it was below the salary earned by my industry peers. I found that I had a hard time "paying myself" what I deserved. My mind generated reasons for this discrepancy: I had been off in the startup world for the past eight years, I didn't want to appear arrogant, I had no recent salary to compare. I struggled with this issue for a number of weeks as I was refining my Living Vision.

Finally, one morning, I got into a dialogue with myself on this question as I was writing in my daily Reinvention Journal. Finally, the confident and enthusiastic part of me stood up and challenged the safe, shy, fearful side: "What have you got to lose? Why not accept the idea that you're worth twice what you used to make ten years ago?"

I was resistant at first. But gradually I decided to give this approach a chance. I decided to double my hoped-for salary in my mind and on my Living Vision document. Over the subsequent weeks and months as I continued to work with my Living Vision, I got comfortable with the idea of earning this salary.

Sure enough, when my new job finally came through, after months of meetings and conversations, it fulfilled most of the qualities that I haddescribed in my Living Vision—and the company offered me the exact amount of money that I had envisioned.

A miracle? I don't think so. What is more likely is that I had been undervaluing myself, and my new employer was simply offering me a salary based on comparable salaries in my industry for people with my background and expertise. It turned out that my intuition was actually more in touch with reality than my fearful and intimidated mind.

That's how the Living Vision process can work. Rather than describe it as making dreams come true, it might be fairer to say that it helps removethe inner uncertainties that we put in our own path to block our success.

Start your Living Vision by creating a quiet, safe space to sit down, undisturbed, for an hour or two. Add to your environment anything that helps you feel relaxed and nurtured: a candle, soft music, a favorite chair or a bright window to sit by. Maybe there is a sweater or a cap that you wear that helps you relax or concentrate. Maybe you have a favorite park bench or a table at a café where you go to do your best work. Do yourself the favor of choosing whatever circumstances you find most pleasing.

You may type on your computer, but if you feel more comfortable writing longhand, by all means use that method. Then set about drafting your Living Vision. It should be expansive, colorful, and enthusiastic. You want your vision to be ambitious, even daring, but at the same time, you want to avoid crafting a dream that is pure wish-fulfillment, a fantasy that is extremely unlikely to manifest. One simple way to navigate between the extremes of too daring and not daring enough is to strive to create a vision that is *50 percent* believable. Write about a life that extends beyond what you are experiencing today, but don't go overboard. Push the boundaries of your comfort zone, and of the way you see yourself today, but don't raise the bar so high that there's no way you could believe in it. It may be a bit tricky to define precisely what "50 percent believable" means to you, but you can use this description as a guideline to the "feel" you want to achieve.

The way I handled the salary issue in my own Living Vision illustrates one approach to the believability challenge. In shaping my vision, I doubled my future salary—a significant leap. But I didn't triple it or quadruple it. Nor did I imagine myself winning the lottery, curing cancer, or launching a company that would enjoy a successful public offering within a year. Those achievements would almost certainly fall into the realm of fantasy. On the other hand, it might be very believable that you could launch a business within a year, make it a success within three years, and sell it or merge with a larger company within five years.

Write your Living Vision in the first person ("I") and in the present tense. This is extremely important. Write *as if the vision has already happened*, and you are writing one year, three years, or five years from now, looking back on the intervening time period and taking stock of your career and life. You really want to be able to let your imagination explore every possibility and to capture those possibilities in detail. Writing in the first person and in the present tense helps program your mind to accept the vision as attainable by tricking it into treating the vision as an accomplishment that has already happened, a *fait accompli*.

Make sure to include every possible angle on this future vision. Focus on the qualitative aspects of your life, paying particular attention to your relationships with yourself and others. Describe how everything feels. This will help anchor the experience of your future success and give you a sense of confidence and inspiration. The more detailed and nuanced your Living Vision is, the more real it will feel to you, and that sense of inner reality will help drive you toward manifesting it in the real world. Your Living Vision should conclude with a positive evaluation of the journey that has taken you to the envisioned moment in the future, and an expression of continued confidence in your ability to sustain and benefit from your reinvented career.

The Living Vision is meant to be a living document. Read and reread it periodically to check in with its message and to see how the vision is being manifested. You may create a number of successive drafts of your Living Vision as you continue to refine your plan.

To illustrate, here are the opening paragraphs of a possible Living Vision written by someone who is planning to be the owner of a successful new business three years hence:

I am loving owning my own business. From an idea, I have manifested a business that is generating 20 percent more income than I was making in my corporate job, and I have the luxury of being totally in control of my day and my business. After working out of my house for the first year, I was doing well enough to expand into a beautiful coworking space downtown, and as my two full-time staff members joined over the past year, we are now looking at moving to a more permanent location.

One of the best things about the business is my relationship with my clients. At first, it was challenging to understand how best to position my services to meet their needs. Even though some of them were contacts that I had from my corporate work, it was an entirely new process dealing with them as an independent service provider. But working with them and figuring out their needs actually helped me better define what I'm offering, and how to be more successful at delivering it.

The best part of my work day is meeting with my two colleagues at the end of each day to do a quick review and status check on all of our deals. I can't believe that we have generated this much business in this short time span. Sure, the income is great, and I am grateful for being secure in the knowledge that I can have my own business and be successful. But the greater benefit is in relationship to my personal life, and how it has transformed everything at home, with my partner and with my kids. It's as if the fog has cleared in my life, and everything is somehow in a much better state of balance. . . .

As new ideas or changes for your Living Vision occur to you, go back and add them. Little by little, your Living Vision will become clearer and more resonant—which means that you will be increasingly able to make the appropriate choices and follow the signs that will lead you to your reinvention.

STRATEGY #17. CONDUCT A SWOT ANALYSIS

You may be familiar with the concept of the SWOT analysis. SWOT stands for Strengths, Weaknesses, Opportunities, and Threats, and a SWOT analysis is a standard management tool for judging whether a certain course of action is worth pursuing. It lets us ponder and weigh each set of elements against another to come up with a smart course of action.

Applying the SWOT analysis to your second-act career plan is a good way to evaluate whether you're pursuing an idea that makes sense. The chart below contains a starter set of SWOT criteria. You can use these criteria to pose and answer questions about a particular job, business opportunity, or project that you are considering. Feel free to add more specifics that make sense for you and to remove or disregard the ones that don't apply. Print out one or more versions of the chart to use as you're piecing together your strategy or reviewing alternative possibilities.

BOOMER REINVENTION WORKSHEET #7	
BOOMER SWOT ANALYSIS	
STRENGTHS	**WEAKNESSES**
• Financially sustainable • Ethically sound • Geographically sensible • Nurturing work environment • Interpersonally rewarding • Flexible schedule • Decision making	• Financially risky • Ethically questionable • Geographically inconvenient • Challenging work environment • Interpersonally strained • Inflexible schedule • Little or no influence
OPPORTUNITIES	**THREATS**
• Serving the community • Personal growth • Professional development support • Personal meaning • Mentoring others • Healthy lifestyle • Travel • Creative expression • Flexible schedule	• Financial risk • Unhealthy schedule or environment • Toxic personalities • Legal liability

Use the SWOT analysis as a barometer to gauge multiple poten-tial ideas. For example, you may be trying to decide between opening up your own business and buying into a franchise operation. Using the SWOT analysis on each will help you focus on what is important to you and help you decide which option better represents the overall work and lifestyle you'll be comfortable with.

STRATEGY #18. MAP YOUR VISION

A mind map is a graphical representation of complex ideas that helps us understand them more clearly, especially the rela-tionships and dependencies of their component parts. Creating a mind map can help you understand how components of an overall idea relate to one another and help you see how you can turn that idea into reality.

There are a number of different mind map configurations that can be used as reinvention tools. I recommend that you consider the following options. I'll illustrate how each could be used to map ideas related to the buying and launching of a fran-chise business.

THE BUBBLE MAP

This is perhaps the most familiar mind map style. A central bub-ble represents the core idea. Satellite bubbles are linked by straight or curved lines to the core idea or to one another, representing the interrelationships among the ideas. MindMeister, LucidChart, Mind-jet, and similar apps let you create beautiful graphical mind maps. But I like to create a bubble map with a whiteboard and colored pens, which I find much faster and more intuitive than using a computer. I snap a picture of the finished bubble map and clip it to a separate note in Evernote or OneNote.

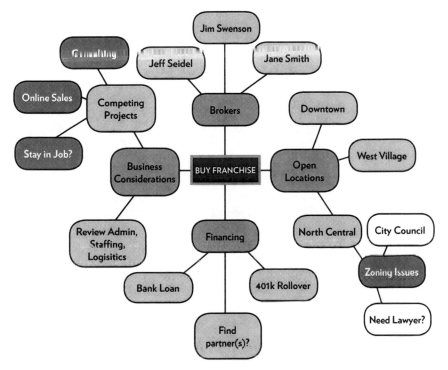

THE STAR MAP

A star map is a simple way of aggregating a set of subsidiary ideas around a central idea. The core concept appears in the middle, and each line in the star map represents a different subsidiary idea. The sample image below, which contains only eight rays, is a simple chart done in Photoshop, but the easiest and most intuitive way of making a star map is with a pen and paper (or on the whiteboard). Draw a small circle in the middle and identify your idea, then just draw rays out from the middle and write your element's description along the ray. Add as many rays as you need (or can fit) to adequately capture all the aspects of the main/core idea. The star map will often be the first tool I use to capture a new idea and all of its aspects without thinking about how those aspects relate to one another. Once I have drawn all the aspects of an idea in a star map, I may move them over to a bubble map and link the bubbles appropriately.

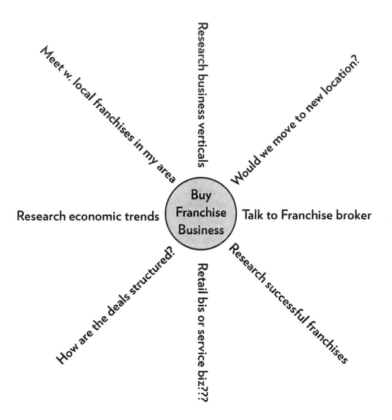

THE LOGIC MAP

The logic map is a text-based approach to help organize ideas around a concept. It's simply a list of answers to the journalist's fundamental questions: Who? What? Where? When? Why? and How? Answering each one of these questions can give you a much clearer idea of how you feel about an idea and what your options are for engaging with it. Logic maps help you to understand priorities and sequences by defining and describing the value of each aspect of the idea. Armed with the answers to these questions, I often will create a subsequent bubble map that charts the interrelationship of the component aspects.

If your word processor has an outline function or view (in MS

Word 2013, for example, it's the View Menu: Outline button), you can use that feature to expand your logic map into an outline. You simply insert subheadings under the appropriate key question. You can also use the worksheet below to create a logic map.

BOOMER REINVENTION WORKSHEET #8	
LOGIC MAP	
Who?	
What?	
Where?	
When?	
Why?	
How?	

Here's an example of how this worksheet might be filled out:

BOOMER REINVENTION WORKSHEET #8	
LOGIC MAP	
Who?	Franchise brokers (Jim, Jeff & Jane) Find the right lawyer to advise me Buy in from the family Talk to my accountant
What?	Which business vertical? Retail or Service? Other considerations?
Where?	Research best neighborhoods Move to new city/state?
When?	Is 6 months realistic? Research time to close deal? Research time to find location, sign lease, construction etc.
Why?	Independence Flexibility Not as much risk Community of Franchisees Support from Franchisor
How?	Take money from 401(k)? Partner with colleagues? Family? Bank loan?

Remember that Evernote and OneNote let you create and sync logic maps across all of your devices. No matter where you are or what device you're using, you are able to open your work and make changes.

THE VISION BOARD

Another mapping technique is the vision board, which is basically a riff on the elaborate collages most of us created in school. A vision board expresses your identity by associating it with pictures, images, and sayings that you might create with your own art supplies or that you could clip from websites, magazines, books, or other sources. Rather than relying exclusively on words, the vision board inspires and appeals to the visual learner inside us.

For example, if you are thinking about opening up a hotel or a restaurant in a resort town, you could create a vision board with images of similar places and locations that inspire you and define the areas you need to focus on: the architecture of storefronts and interiors, lighting and color design, furniture and interior design, kitchen equipment, bedroom accessories, bath accessories, snow-capped mountains for a ski resort, a sunny beach for a seaside resort, and so on. Quotations from famous chefs and hoteliers could also be included.

You can create a vision board by hand, using scissors, paper, and glue, or digitally with the help of a computer. The online image clipping platform Pinterest serves many of the same functions as a vision board and can certainly be used in this way, but it does not allow the freeform layout and placement of elements that can make a handmade vision board particularly creative and lively.

Mind maps of all kinds are valuable tools for you to use at every stage of your reinvention process. As you get ideas about what your reinvention could entail, you can use a mind map to explore them and refine them. If your idea is to, for example, stay at your present company and figure out a better role for yourself, you could create two star maps, each with the company name at the center of the map. In map A, you would add rays to describe your current situation at the company; in map B, you would add rays to describe your hoped-for situation at the company. Map A would be the "before" vision, and map B would be the "after" vision.

TROUBLESHOOTING: WHAT IF YOU'RE STUCK?

"Resistance is futile" was the infamous motto of the Borg Collective, the seemingly unstoppable evil alien cyborg race on *Star Trek*. Yet as we've noted, inner resistance is a very common phenomenon for those who are working the reinvention process. If you are getting stuck in your efforts to navigate any of the Expressing step strategies, try the following:

- Stop beating yourself up. Many people who launch the reinvention process are discouraged from previous attempts to figure out their second-act careers or get more traction in the job market. As a result, they tend to beat themselves up, blaming themselves for their failures and becoming increasingly depressed and demotivated. If this happens to you, go back to the affirmation process in the Accepting step and create a new, positive affirmation—something along the lines of, "I am gently supporting myself to recharge and reinvigorate my career, taking one step at a time, and taking credit for each win, no matter how small."

- Print out a few small copies of the affirmation and tape them up in locations where you'll see them often: your bedside table, your fridge, your bathroom mirror, and your computer screen. Be aware of them throughout the day. Repeat them when you can. It may take a month or so for the message to sink in, but you will eventually begin to see progress.

- Go visual. Buy a Post-It Easel Pad or any similar large-format pad of sticky poster sheets. Draw a big monthly calendar on a sheet and tack it up where you're going to see it every day at least once. Every day that you complete at least one of your four

Expressing strategies, mark the date with a big X. Don't underestimate the power of seeing your progress in graphic terms.

- Set recurring appointments and reminders in your phone and/ or your calendar. Decide which days of the week you're going to work on your reinvention process. Then create and record those appointments as if you were meeting with an important client or having a check-in meeting with your boss.

- Underwhelm yourself. Start small and set very light expectations. Choose one thirty-minute block of time per week and start there. Use that time to do any one of the four Expressing strategies. That's your success for the week.

- Create a ritual. Pick an action that is easy to do, has no emotional charge to it (that is, it doesn't trigger any negative thoughts), and is unrelated to your reinvention process. It could be reading a book, working in the garden, or some other nurturing activity (but *not* browsing Facebook or some other online distraction!). Whenever you are feeling resistant or unable to focus, pick up that activity for thirty minutes and see how you feel. Shifting your attention away from your reinvention plan will likely relax your mind, take some of the pressure off you, and give the ideas and positive steps the opportunity to float into your awareness. You will likely begin to think about your reinvention process after five or ten minutes. Keep a little notepad or 3x5 card with you and jot down any ideas you're not going to want to forget. At the end of your thirty minutes, you'll probably have a list of a few reinvention actions you are interested in and willing to do.

- Reboot. Don't think you have to stick with a specific second-act career choice just because you've gotten pretty far down the road with it. If you are starting to accumulate doubts about a plan, don't be afraid to go back to the beginning and start again. So what if you end up "wasting" a month or two with an idea that fizzles out? Maybe you needed to commit to that weaker idea and play it out as far as you could in order to realize it wasn't really for you. I know people who have gone through two or three reboots in their reinvention process. Losing two, three, or six months following a dead end is nothing compared to the ten or twenty years you've got in front of you to thrive in your second-act career.

Taking one step back to take two steps forward is a perfectly acceptable idea. Don't feel obligated to be constantly making the same rate of forward progress.

ACKNOWLEDGE YOURSELF

In the fifth and final step of the Boomer Reinvention process, you will gather up everything you have created in the Expressing step and take it out into the world. But first, if you haven't taken the time to acknowledge what you've done and feel good about yourself, now is the time to do it. Emerging from the Expressing step with a clear idea of where you want to go in your second-act career is a massive accomplishment.

It is time to celebrate and share your vision for where you are going. While you have likely been sharing your progress with your family and close friends, why not throw a party for yourself to give those who are rooting for you the chance to cheer you on as you prepare to go public with your plan? Hold a brunch, a dinner, or a cocktail party at home, at a friend's home, or at a bar or a restaurant, and invite the people who mean the most to you. They have likely been with you as you have worked through all the steps of the process.

Think of this as your coming-out party. It is the point from which you are launching yourself out into the world in a new or augmented way. Use the gathering as your own personal pep rally—building your self-confidence and basking in the support of those who are in your corner.

There is a certain amount of vulnerability involved in taking this step. You are baring your soul and trusting yourself in unknown territory. This gathering strengthens your commitment to yourself and will inspire your supporters to continue to work with you as you embark on the fifth and final step of the Boomer Reinvention methodology.

Chapter 14

CONNECTING:
THE PROOF IS IN
THE PEOPLE

EXPRESSING WHAT YOU WANT TO DO in your second-act career is all well and good, but manifesting that plan is where the proverbial rubber meets the road. That's where the Connecting step comes in.

As we've discussed, a lot has changed about getting a job or starting a business in the wake of the digital revolution. The good news is that software and connectivity have made it easier and faster for a job seeker to find people, research companies, apply for open positions, share referrals and recommendations, and provide links to past accomplishments. They also make it easier for aspiring entrepreneurs to investigate market conditions, secure financing, set up operations, connect with potential partners, and outsource administrative functions.

The bad news is that those of us born in an analog age who haven't kept up with these developments have a lot to learn. It is easy to get lost in all of the choices and options now available for turning your plan into a reality.

In the Connecting step, I'll suggest five strategies for cutting through the confusion and realizing the career plan you developed in the Expressing step. The goal is not only near-term career success but also the creation of a trusted system you can use to sustain that career and allow it to evolve in response to changing conditions, your own growth, and new opportunities.

STRATEGY #19. TURN YOUR NETWORK INTO A CAREER RELATIONSHIP FUNNEL

"Chase relationships, not job openings." This is a mantra I share with my graduate students as well as with my boomer clients. It represents a paradigm shift away from thinking that career development is mainly about distributing résumés to apply for open positions. In the digital age, we all have to be more proactive about creating and nurturing a network of strategic business relationships that will get us in the door before the job opening is even posted. This also applies to business creation, where we need potential investors to know us and trust us before we ask them for a penny.

Trying to land a job or start a business without a preexisting network today is like trying to win a war without an army. If you are not part of an active network, your chances of landing a job, raising money for a venture, or finding any of the resources you'll need to further your career are significantly diminished.

Most people have a fuzzy sense of what it means to have an active network. A network is not simply your contact list or address book, your Facebook friends, your former colleagues, your college classmates, or the members of your union, guild, or professional association. These are all important people, and many of them could help you get a job or locate the resources that will help you launch your business. But the fact that you know them and can reach them doesn't necessarily make them part of an active network.

An active network consists of people who can make a strategic contribution that will serve to advance your career goals. It can help you not only to get a job or to start a business but also to *maintain* a successful job or business. Your active network funnels new ideas, new people, and new business opportunities to you.

In order to activate your contact list for that purpose, you need to figure out who to focus on and how to interact with them. An active network takes managing. That's because an active network is a two-way street. Not only are you seeking help from the people who support you, you are also providing support for them in whatever they are doing. In giving you will receive. In fact, I encourage you to engage with your network primarily as a giver of encouragement, expertise, empathy, insight, support, and information, and only secondarily as a receiver of help (including job referrals).

If you are perceived as someone who is giving of their time, energy, knowledge, and other resources, people will look forward to hearing from you because you will usually be offering them something: an article you just read, a valuable experience you wanted to share, a suggestion based on a conversation with a colleague, or an introduction to someone they might enjoy connecting with.

Contrast that with someone who only gets in touch when they need something: they want to know if you've heard of any job openings; they are looking for the names of people who might have open positions and want you to refer them. It's all one way—their way. They never have anything to offer. Their attitude is a bit desperate. They come across as needy.

So when you network, don't lead with your need.

If someone asks you how you're doing at a time when you are struggling in your career, you don't have to hide or gloss over your predicament, but you can address the question positively: "Well, things could be better. I'm still looking for a job. But I've been very active, learning a bunch of new things, meeting a bunch of new people, and I feel positive about my search. In the long run, I know I'm going to land someplace great."

This may be challenging for you to do, but it is essential in order to maintain the positive flow of information from your network. When you communicate with people in a positive way, focusing on what you can give rather than what you hope to receive, they will be uplifted when they hear from you. They will also be inspired to return the favor when they come across an appropriate job opening or another way they can help you.

Over time, your active network can serve as a lead generation system that is very similar to a classic marketing funnel. Here's how it works.

Start by dividing all the contacts in your database into three groups—Platinum, Gold, and Silver.

Your Platinum group is your smallest group. It may include only a handful of people—but they are vitally important. They are your de facto "board of directors," the people with whom you are closest and with whom you can really let your hair down and be vulnerable. They love you and support you no matter what, have confidence in you, and are the most committed to your success. They may include family, close friends, long-time business colleagues, and fellow school alumni. They also have the strategic vision and management skills to guide you effectively toward your career goals. For example, they may have the right kind of experience to help you secure a key job interview, negotiate a crucial deal, or deal with a problem person at work. They are people with whom you can talk about your career goals and practice your job interview skills. They are compassionate, encouraging, and have your best interests at heart; they are not people who can't wait to tell you what you're doing wrong or why they know more than you do.

If there's no one in your life now who matches this description of a Platinum contact, don't worry. That's not unusual. You may be able to turn a few members of your Gold group into the nucleus of a Platinum group.

Your Gold group includes everyone with whom you have a good working relationship—people who are, at the very least, "in your corner." They are like-minded individuals who may or may not work in the same field as you. You may have done business with them as coworker, client, or vendor. You may know them socially or through your community activities. Consider which of these Gold group members you can approach to discuss your career reinvention plan and how best to engage with each of them. If you are interested in shifting your career to a new field, perhaps some of your Gold group can make introductions for you or suggest information or training resources. If you are looking to expand your reach in your existing field, there may be Gold group members who can help you do that.

It's possible that some members of your Gold group are both trustworthy enough and strategic enough to become part of your Platinum group. Review your Gold list and identify candidates who may be appropriate for this kind of "promotion."

To test the waters with a Gold contact who might be suitable as a Platinum contact, you don't even have to tell them about your networking strategy. Just start opening up to them slowly about your situation and your reinvention plan, and ask them if they would be willing to spend some time helping you. You'll discover quickly whether or not your assessment of them was correct. Not everyone will be willing to support you in your reinvention effort, nor will everyone bring the right mix of skills, experience, or insight to the task. Nor will everyone have the right personality type. After all, you want to feel positive and energized when you talk to them, not discouraged or judged.

If someone in your Gold group proves unworthy of joining your Platinum group, that's okay. The Gold group is a very valuable cohort just as it is.

Your Silver group is the largest, most general group. These are the people you've met who have the potential to be members of your Gold group. They are people whose business cards you have collected at networking events, conferences, or business meetings; friends of friends who have asked to join your network on LinkedIn; colleagues present or former whom you barely know but whom you could call or email based on shared connections.

Periodically review the names in your Silver list. Look for opportunities to draw closer to the ones with whom you sense you may have the potential for a deeper connection. Based on shaking hands, having a quick conversation, and learning more about what they do, you'll know whether or not they merit a follow-up coffee or a lunch meeting to get to know them better. If the "simpatico" appears to be working, you'll likely be able to start working with them as a member of your Gold group.

Thus, networking contacts start out as Silver, progress to Gold, and in a few special cases wind up as Platinum. Your life and career are fluid, so your network will be, too. Your Gold and Platinum contacts may change when you get a new job or start a new business and need to develop a different set of resources. Equally as important, you will also participate as a Silver, Gold, or Platinum member of other people's networks.

Your three-level collection of contacts serves as your career relationship funnel. It helps you to find and develop relationships with people who think as you do, appreciate what you have to offer, are grateful for the assistance and support you provide for them, and are willing to connect you to job openings, people who can hire you, or people who will help you launch your own business. Building and continually nurturing this funnel is a key element in the Expressing step of the Boomer Reinvention methodology.

STRATEGY #20. OPTIMIZE YOUR PROFILE(S)

Just as dating has scaled up from personal introductions and mixer events to online dating sites, business relationships have scaled, too. Local in-person networking is still invaluable, and I encourage you to avail yourself of all opportunities to meet new people in your immediate area— professional associations, labor unions, church groups, community groups, business conferences, chamber of commerce events, lodges, and so on. But the real action in building a network today is online. The scale and global reach of the internet means that by engaging with people in this larger context, you will have greater access to the fabled six degrees of connection between you and literally anyone else on the planet.

In particular, business today has become all about social networking. Over the last ten years, social media has become a distinctive cultural and economic paradigm that is impossible to ignore. Indeed, 73 percent of millennials report that they found their jobs through social networks.

However, many of us boomers have adopted social media without fully embracing it or understanding its value. Many persist in the notion that social media is for younger generations or that it is purely for recreation. You may have believed that spending the time to learn social media for professional purposes was a nice-to-have, not a must-have. Now it's time to change that attitude. If you're now engaged in reinventing and repositioning your career, you absolutely cannot ignore social media.

One of the ways social media has impacted our career process is by rendering the résumé almost obsolete. Remember that the typical recruiter or hiring manager spends about seven seconds skimming your résumé—if they read it at all. In larger companies, résumés get scanned electronically for keywords before being reviewed by a human. In fact, there are services that will help you revise your résumé to include the keywords companies are looking for in those scans. But your résumé is essentially a reference tool, not a marketing tool. It will be used by recruiters and hiring managers once you're in the door and going around to interview within the organization. At that stage in the process, it becomes the cheat-sheet that company managers use to track you in their hiring process.

So stop fussing and fretting over your résumé. Yes, it needs to be current, accurate, and well-formatted as well as complete, authentic, and transparent. But spend less of your time focusing on your résumé and more on creating a consistent and authoritative online presence, including a set of carefully crafted profiles across all the most appropriate social media platforms. This is where employers, clients, customers, and partners will discover you, research your background, and learn about who you are, how you operate, and how you think.

YOUR LINKEDIN PROFILE IS CRUCIAL

LinkedIn has become a unique constellation in the social media galaxy. With (as of 2017) north of four hundred million users in two hundred countries, it has become arguably the most effective large-scale business networking platform, as well as the primary job-seeking, recruiting, and hiring tool in the U.S.

If you don't have an active presence on LinkedIn, starting with a full profile and professional headshot, then get busy. Our generation can't afford to ignore this colossal resource. Studies have found that posting a professional headshot on LinkedIn makes you fourteen times more likely to be found by a recruiter, while listing skills in your profile multiplies your chances by thirteen times.

Filling in a complete LinkedIn profile means treating it just like your résumé—except that LinkedIn's format allows you to actually include more information than you would be able to include in a two-page résumé.

The key concept here is "search." Like pretty much every destination on the internet, LinkedIn is one colossal search engine, and in order to be found on LinkedIn, you have to optimize your profile around keywords that define and describe you. By now, after participating in all of the Expressing step strategies, you should be able to create a list of words that fit your sense of who you are, what you are looking to do, and where and how you are looking to do it. Refine that list down to a handful of keywords that you will incorporate throughout your profile.

In my LinkedIn profile, for example, you'll notice the words "reinvention," "career," and "coach" a lot, along with "boomer," "midlife," "career development," and a few more. I crammed three of them into my headline: "reinvention career coach." This identifies my job description and also helps me surface in searches, especially when people are searching for a career coach. If I had separated the words "career" and "coach," for example, by listing myself as a "career reinvention coach," I would have diluted my intended search results.

Your keywords need to hook you into existing categories where people will be searching and work synergistically to show your unique mix of skills, experience, and intention.

Here are some other must-do steps in optimizing your LinkedIn profile:

- Upload a professional-quality color headshot. You want people to be able to recognize you from your headshot when they meet you in person, so choose and edit your photo accordingly. It should show just you, fill the frame, be well lit, and should capture your authenticity and positive attitude.
- Pack all your keywords into the professional headline, making it as precise and laser-targeted as possible. This is how you want to be searched for, so imagine how you would compose a Google search if you were looking for you.
- The summary is arguably the most important section of your LinkedIn profile. It has to draw the reader in right away and inspire them to add you to their contacts. Notice that the section expands when a reader clicks it; therefore, the key purpose of your first few lines is to pull the reader in and get them to expand the section and read your entire story. Pepper this section with keywords as well.
- Fill out your complete timeline. Don't leave out any time period on the assumption that people aren't interested or won't bother to scroll through your entire history. As with your résumé, omitting any periods of time from your profile

will only raise suspicions. Of course, you can and should put the best spin on your history, so, for example, you could combine a number of contiguous jobs or consulting deals under one heading. If you were out of work for longer than three months at any time, consider listing that period as a consultancy, preferably one in the same field as the job you eventually got. This conveys a certain sense of continuity and strategy: you developed traction in a given area, and then were hired "in-house" in that area. And if you have spent a period as a caregiver—as a parent, or possibly *for* a parent—list it the way you would list any job, including responsibilities and achievements (project management, fund-raising, scheduling, and conflict resolution). This fits the way our society is gradually learning to view caregiving as a professional responsibility like any other.

As we've discussed earlier, it's important to be completely open about your age and your experience. Don't waste your time or the time of others trying to represent yourself as something you're not. If someone is ageist, they will probably reject you when they meet you anyway—and fudging your age in your profile isn't going to help.

THE POWER OF LINKEDIN GROUPS

LinkedIn groups are an extremely powerful resource. There are well over two million interest groups on the platform, and you can join as many as one hundred of them. A group can represent a small niche or a major industry with tens of thousands of members. Whatever you do, have done, or want to do, there will likely be a group that you can join that will be helpful for your career.

Be strategic about your group strategy. Join groups that cover all the bases:

- Groups with potential employers, including recruiters and executive search firms

- Groups with potential clients
- Groups with potential career allies, including people just like you who may be looking for a job, may have recently found a job, or who might refer you for a job
- Groups with people who can help you start your business, coach you, or be suppliers, partners, or customers for your startup

Once you have explored the ways in which you can set up LinkedIn to your advantage, you can work on growing your network. You can take advantage of LinkedIn's search functionality by narrowing down the characteristics of people you are searching for. You can search by zip code, industry, job title, sector, age, seniority level, and interests, among other criteria. This makes it easy to zero in on just the kinds of people who would be most interested in hiring you, funding you, partnering with you, or referring you. To maximize your access to all of these search functions, you will need to invest in a paid subscription to LinkedIn. It's well worth the money.

When you visit someone's LinkedIn profile, they will see that you have visited them and will be able to check out who you are. If they visit you back, that is a likely indication that they are at least interested in learning more about who you are and that they may be open to entering into a more in-depth conversation, today or in the future.

Playing this "I viewed you and you viewed me" game enables you to grow your connections list on LinkedIn. Send a connection request to those you'd like to meet, but rather than just clicking the Connect button, navigate to their profile. Using the dropdown arrow to the right of the Connect and Send Inmail buttons, click the menu item labeled "connect." This will open up a dialogue where you can send them a message, which is an effective and personal way to connect. Check the "friend" button in response to the "How do you know them" question, and enter a brief message along the lines of, "I see you visited my profile earlier. It appears we have a number of things in common [elaborate briefly if you like]. It would be a pleasure to connect here on LinkedIn." You'll have to keep the message brief, as you only have a limited number of characters available, but being personal increases the odds you will got accepted as a connection.

Yes, reaching out to people in this way can be time-consuming. But if you devote thirty to sixty minutes per day to this activity, you may wind up with twenty, thirty, or more new connections per week, all narrowly targeted leads who may be of value to your plan. As appropriate, you can create opportunities to meet them in person, whether one-on-one or at a local networking or business event where you can meet and discuss your shared interests and ambitions. And don't forget that your primary role is to be a giver, not a taker. Your reputation and your credibility will grow in direct proportion to the degree in which you are seen as helpful, supportive, informative, and insightful.

STRATEGY #21. BECOME A THOUGHT LEADER

A thought leader is someone with opinions shaped by experience, interaction, and critical thinking and who is known for the way they articulate their particular point of view. In our connected, social-media-dominated world, engaging as a thought leader by publishing blog posts and comments is a great way to stand out in a competitive career marketplace.

You qualify as a potential thought leader for the simple reason that you have been around for a long time and have done a lot of things. You likely have a lot more to say than you realize. Remember how John Pugliano, the sales executive turned financial advisor, started a successful podcast because he was frustrated that no one was expressing his particular point of view on a particular development—so he took matters in to his own hands. By sharing your ideas, you create reasons to start conversations with other people. It's another opportunity to be a giver rather than a taker, providing helpful information and advice from your experience and drawing people to you in the process.

Thought leadership is a very attainable goal. When I started my reinvention career coaching practice for boomers, I knew relatively little about the challenges facing our generation beyond the headlines and some of the statistics. Determined to become an expert in this area, I began reading everything I could get my hands on. I read books and articles and subscribed to blogs of people who were writing about this topic.

Over time, I began to form opinions about the material I was reading, shaped by my research as well as by my own experiences and observations. I found that there were experts I generally agreed with and others I disagreed with. I saw that some organizations in the space had orientations and visions that were compatible with my own, while others didn't.

Finally, I began to post comments on people's blogs, including on sites like *Huffington Post* and *Forbes,* and especially on LinkedIn groups. As I got more comfortable, I found that more and more ideas would come to me, and I began compiling notes for what eventually became my own blog posts.

For John Pugliano, with no prior background in the financial services industry, his blog served as an expression of his market analyses and predictions. John didn't have to sell prospective clients on his abilities: all they had to do was read what he had written three, six, or twelve months previously to realize that this was a guy who knew what he was talking about and whose expertise might make him a valuable investment advisor. John, in short, had become a thought leader.

If you begin to engage intelligently with your network online, you will develop a reputation based on the helpful and informative contributions you make in your subject area. That reputation helps define you as someone unique in a way that the simple listing of jobs and accomplishments on your résumé or online profile can never accomplish.

Your ability to take a proactive role as a thought leader also gives you plenty to talk about with your network. This means that you are never at a loss when calling someone up or sending them a message. It will also prompt others to contact you in order to comment on what you have shared or to ask you a question based on what you know.

Not everyone is going to agree with what you post. By engaging actively, you will find out who your ideas resonate with and who disagrees with you. You will quickly find the people with whom you share various affinities, and these are the people you want to continue to cultivate. Don't waste time trying to convert people to your cause. If some eventually come around, so much the better. But focus your interactions primarily on the people who are strategic and who align with your point of view.

DEVELOPING YOUR PLATFORM

While LinkedIn will probably be your primary business contact and networking resource, you can also use other social media platforms to engage with like-minded peers, prospective clients, employers, partners, and friends. This activity creates a virtual online footprint for you that becomes your personal platform.

The choice of sites on which you'll build your platforms defines your priorities and preferences. There are many sites for you to investigate and consider. By experimenting and spending some time on the ones that seem to be in the ballpark, you'll develop a sense of which ones are appropriate for you and you'll narrow your participation accordingly. Be selective—you don't have to spend all your time on social media!

In Expressing, I referenced the image-clipping site Pinterest. You may choose to use Pinterest to support your business because of the kinds of people you meet there and the specific ways in which what you post resonates with them.

Most boomers use Facebook to stay in touch with friends. But having a business page on Facebook may be a good way for you to engage with customers or to post interesting updates or articles that relate to your business.

A lot of people hang out on Reddit and participate in active online discussions there. Others like answering questions on Quora. Some businesses are posting regularly on Instagram. If you've got a lot to share during the course of the day, you might want to use Twitter. Your choice depends on what works for you and your business.

Whatever social media sites you choose, you'll engage in five core practices that will help you build and nurture your thought leadership platform: collecting content, following people, publishing posts, sharing content, and engaging others.

1.   Collecting content is the research phase of the thought leadership process. Here is where you will lay the groundwork for your personal branding and messaging. Receiving constant input and information about your chosen area(s) of expertise will help you form opinions and a point of view you can share. Use tools like Google Alerts and subscriptions to RSS feeds from websites you value to receive regular input. If you find that you are overwhelmed with updates, use the service http://unroll. me to consolidate all of your subscriptions into one daily email digest. And don't forget to include your own name to track the mentions you may receive in the press or elsewhere online.

2.   Following people involves subscribing to updates directly from the people who you find most influential in your field. Follow them on the social media platforms they publish on, including Facebook, Twitter, LinkedIn, Instagram, and others. This is a way to actually engage with them directly by replying to their posts, and even alerting them and linking to your own posts or updates. I have developed more than a few business relationships through the process of following and being followed on Twitter or LinkedIn.

3.   Publishing blog posts is the core of your thought leadership practice. As you study the material you're collecting, you will naturally begin to form opinions that can find expression as blog posts. Typically blog posts run anywhere from five hundred to seven hundred words, the equivalent of one or two typed pages. There are innumerable online resources to help you create, format, and optimize your posts, covering themes like how to choose a topic, structure the post, and draft a catchy headline.

You don't have to go to the trouble of creating your own separate blog—at least not right away. Instead, you can post to one or more of the many blog sites (most of them free), including Medium and Wordpress. You can also post blogs on LinkedIn. The bigger blog sites like *Huffington Post* and *Forbes* typically require an application and audition process. Other sites are open to publishing "guest posts" from individual bloggers. If you are posting regularly and consistently and focusing on a clear and specific topic, this will qualify you to guest-post for other sites and to be accepted as a contributor by the larger sites.

Eventually, if you develop a following for your online writing and if you are enjoying writing enough to turn out blog posts frequently (several times a week or more), you may want to launch your own personal blog. Former publisher Michael Hyatt has become a prolific resource for people looking to start their own blogs. You can check out his insights at http:// michaelhyatt.com.

4.   The fourth thought leadership practice is sharing content. As you read articles and information from various sources, you will want to share the most significant pieces with your connections and followers across the sites that are part of your platform—i.e., with what has become your community. This process has come to be known as content curation. Like a curator in a gallery or a museum, you are looking at the totality of the available content in your chosen field and distilling it down into small bites geared to your audience and reflective of your own point of view. You can streamline and automate and schedule the process of posting the same piece of information to multiple sites. Check out publishing tools like Tweetdeck, Buffer, and Hootsuite.

Sharing content in this way helps build your authority and helps get you noticed and recognized as a thought leader. Don't just post a link to the update; comment on it and provide the reason and the context for why you're sharing it. In this way, people will begin to understand your point of view, seek out and follow your writings, and share them with their own networks.

Don't overshare. Balance quality and quantity. Each social media site has its own most effective practices, and by engaging with others on your preferred sites you'll figure out how frequently to post: not so rarely that you're not really a presence, but not so often that people start to tune you out. You'll know how effective you are by the number of responses—"likes" on Facebook or shares that you get on each piece. Over time, you'll begin to get a sense of what your audience really likes, which can vary depending on the platform.

5.   The fifth thought leadership practice is to engage other people by making a comment on something you've read (including from the people you follow), whether on a social media platform, on a newspaper or magazine website, or in the comment section following an article that you find through Google Alerts. This is a fine way to seed new potential relationships and make your presence known wherever there is something being written about that relates to your area of expertise.

Responding to comments on your own posts and updates can create new networking relationships for your contact funnel and seed potential business opportunities. Remember, of course, that unless you are using private email, all of your communications with your online social media contacts are public. So be thoughtful about your tone and your vocabulary. I try to keep my comments and postings brief, upbeat, and positive. At some point, one or more people on the internet will likely try to lure you into a negative conversation, or try to insult you or belittle your message ("trolling"). Don't be tempted to engage with them, as nothing good can come of it. You have to stay above the fray.

As you build your thought leadership reputation, your perceived expertise and the engagement of your friends and followers will translate into meetings, interviews, new connections, and other opportunities throughout your contact funnel.

STRATEGY #22. SHINE IN EVERY MEETING

The Intern (2015), starring Robert De Niro, is a lighthearted comedy about a retired widower who is bored with hanging out with the same boomers he's known for years. So he signs on as an intern for a millennial-run internet retail startup. He winds up mentoring his young boss, played by Anne Hathaway, helping her straighten out her company and her life. Sure, it's a Hollywood movie with the happy ending, but the jokes and the situations all ring true, and the movie winds up being a great template for how reinvented boomers can triumph in the workplace.

At this point in the Boomer Reinvention process, it's time to get out there in the real (not virtual) world and develop the new relationships that are going to help you get to where you want to go. In this strategy, I'll offer some advice about how to make your meetings with new people positive, productive, and valuable both for you and for the people you meet.

When you head into a meeting of any kind—a job interview, an introduction to a new contact, or a meeting to discuss ongoing business—you'll want to take advantage of the situation and make it work for you.

Be 100 percent engaged and enthusiastic for whatever you are doing, but 100 percent detached from the outcome. This is wise advice I received from a mentor that I've found extraordinarily valuable over the years. It's a reminder that, win or lose, the outcome of today's meeting is ultimately out of your control. You can only be the best person you can be—and that is enough.

Choose to be self-confident and positive. You don't have to sell too hard or justify yourself, but showing your confident side always increases the chance that the meeting will be fruitful for everyone involved. If you're having a hard time finding your confidence and your equanimity, think back to a time in your life and your career when things were really humming on all cylinders. Remember that feeling and bring it forward. Then breathe and smile.

Be oriented toward the future, not the past. Your experience, sad to say, is not as valued as it once was or as it should be. After all, in today's fast-changing world, experience may not help with conquering a completely out-of-left-field challenge. So instead of talking about your experience, demonstrate that you're curious, adaptable, open, resourceful, creative, and persistent. It will become clear to those you meet with that your life and work experience is a gift to be appreciated rather than a badge that demands homage.

In many meetings, you're going to find yourself being one of the oldest people in the room. People will respond to that according to their own biases (which of course is always true no matter what life stage you are in). You may notice people are looking at you differently in meetings. That look runs the gamut from respect and interest to awkwardness and defensiveness. What matters most is how you respond.

As we've discussed throughout this book, ageism is a reality you need to be prepared to deal with. There is a mountain of evidence debunking the most commonly held prejudices about age, some of which I refer to in Chapter 2. It can be helpful to study all of this valuable information, but be careful about using it defensively. Rather than try to educate younger people about the folly of ageism, or otherwise stand stubbornly in resistance and defiance to the injustice of this bias, take a more strategic course of action.

My advice: ignore any bias you encounter. Roll right over it. Show by your attitude (rather than stating in words) that you have absolutely no problems dealing with younger people. Remember that you're not there to teach them a lesson, you're not there to tell them war stories about how things were when you were their age, and you're not there to impress them with how much you've learned and grown over the years. Instead, you're there to be of service and of value in that meeting. So use your gist thinking abilities to listen thoroughly, and then respectfully propose a solution or a pathway forward in response to whatever challenge or problem the group is tackling. It's amazing how a few small shifts in attitude can produce amazing results. Following this strategy can ensure that, rather than being perceived as a distant know-it-all, you'll be viewed and valued as an accessible solution provider.

STRATEGY #23. ACE EVERY JOB INTERVIEW

The job interview is its own particular subset of a meeting, and you can benefit from some additional practices to do your best and set it up for success. Yes, it is awkward to realize and to contemplate that most of the people who will be interviewing you are going to be younger than you are. But if you are willing to, as in the previous strategy, roll over that detail, you may find that your positive and service-oriented attitude (after all, you are there to help them solve some sort of problem) might just win the day.

First, remember to be transparent—willing to reveal things that you might feel a little uncomfortable about. Don't hedge your way through questions like, "Why did you leave your last position?" or "How long have you been looking for a job?" Remember Strategies #10 and #11. Your discomfort may be taken as a sign that you aren't right for the position. Spend time prepping for these questions and find answers that are honest and authentic, showing that you are willing and able to acknowledge and overcome challenges and to learn from the experiences. This may be a great opportunity to inject some self-deprecating humor into the conversation. A little vulnerability can go a long way toward creating empathy and respect for what you've been through.

It's not about you; it's about the fit. At the end of the day, the outcome of your interview has about 10 percent to do with your résumé and about 90 percent to do with fit. Does the interviewer think you're someone that everyone else is going to enjoy coming to work with? In today's flattened-hierarchy organizations, hiring and firing are more team-driven than ever, so don't take it personally if you must participate in a half dozen rounds of interviews with all the stakeholders you could be working with. Think about it this way: if there's no fit, do you really want to be working with a team that doesn't understand and appreciate you for who you are?

Interview them. Be curious. Do your homework. They actually want to see that you're engaged. So ask perceptive questions to show that you understand not only the job but also the company and the culture. The point is not to be arrogant or to try to take over the interview. Instead, get into a real conversation. Use your questions and the thoughtful two-way discussion that ensues to reveal why you could indeed be the right fit for this job.

Finally, remember that follow-up never gets old. While so much has changed in the hiring process, the fundamental things still apply (as Dooley Wilson sang in *Casablanca*). Remember to thank your interviewer by email immediately (within the hour, from your smartphone!). And just like in the old days, send a handwritten thank-you note the same day. In fact, I advise clients to actually have the note card in their pocket or bag all ready to go, with a stamp already affixed. No matter how old or young your interviewer is, he or she will be impressed with your follow-up. It may not get you the job, but it demonstrates your thoughtfulness and your character. That's how you roll. . . .

Epilogue
REINVENTION YOUR WAY

The worksheets featured in this book are available for download by registering on the Boomer Reinvention website at http://boomer reinvention.com or by scanning the QR code on this page.

Career reinvention is a process. In this book, the five steps and twenty-three strategies have been laid out in a logical order from inner process to outer manifestation. But we know that life isn't always quite so orderly. You can certainly follow the steps and the strategies in sequence, and I expect that you'll have a valuable experience as a result. But I also encourage you to follow the system at your own pace and in your own way. Start with what feels most comfortable or most immediate—the steps and strategies that best apply to where you are right now. Then try more strategies as needed. They may work very differently for you depending on where you already are in your career when you pick up the book.

For reference, here is a table with all five steps and twenty-three strategies:

BOOMER REINVENTION WORSHEET #9				
23 REINVENTION STRATEGIES				
Reframing	Strategy #1. Assess the Status Quo	Strategy #2. Reframe the Personal and the Local	Strategy #3. Reframe Limiting Roles – or: You Are More than Your Resume	Strategy #4. Act "As If"	Strategy #5. Reframe Your Mission
Listening	Strategy #6 Perform Basic Research	Strategy #7 Solicit Feed-back	Strategy #8 Adopt New Ways of Listening	Strategy #9 Be of Service	
Accepting	Strategy #10 Reconcile Your Resume	Strategy #11 Stop Being A Victim	Strategy #12 Reclaim Your Identity	Strategy #13 Practice Empathy Rather Than Sympathy	Strategy #14 Create Your Affirmation
Expressing	Strategy #15 Keep a Reinvention Journal	Strategy # 16 Create a Living Vision	Strategy #17 Conduct a SWOT Analysis	Strategy #18 Map Your Vision	
Connecting	Strategy #19 Turn Your Network Into a Career Relationship Funnel	Strategy #20 Optimize Your Profile(s)	Strategy #21 Become a Thought Leader	Strategy #22 Shine in Every Meeting	Strategy #23 Ace Every Job Interview

This table is also available on the book website, along with a version that can be printed out on a note card for handy reference at any time in your day, or clipped to your Evernote or OneNote app.

THE REINVENTED BOOMERS & THE BOOMER REINVENTION STEPS

Here are brief summaries of how each of the boomers profiled in Part II used the five steps to their advantage.

JOHN PUGLIANO

Reframing: John realized that he wanted to be the millionaire next door rather than following the traditional white-collar career executive path. He also changed his mind about the financial services sector and realized that he didn't have to be part of the "dirty industry" to be successful as a financial advisor.

Listening: John avoided listening for so long . . . he didn't listen to his "inner" voice. But people did seek him out for his expertise—and he finally took his wife's feedback, even though it was difficult to do, and that forced him to work through his resistance and start his advisory business.

Accepting: John figured out that he wasn't interested in the same values and material goals as the other executives he was working with, and that he wasn't the white-collar executive that his mother wanted him to be. He also realized that the perfect job is not "out there," and that he was not only okay with that but could really embrace the entrepreneur within.

Expressing: John strategized his stock-trading plan and continued to explore and be open to planning his career, visualizing his life, and deciding which niche he was going to serve.

Connecting: John started to blog, using social media to express his authenticity and to identify and pursue his clientele. His realization that he had something to say about his industry prompted his first podcast, and the subsequent growth of his audience has made him a significant thought leader.

JUDY CONTRERAS

Reframing: Judy was willing to take a long hard look at her HR career and realize that it no longer held the promise that it once held for her. As a result, she was willing to look at doing something entirely different.

Listening: The work Judy did with her Small Business Administration (SBA) mentor was crucial in giving her the confidence to make her move into being a broker/consultant.

Accepting: Even though Judy was on track to buy into a franchise business, she was perceptive enough to finally figure out that this wasn't for her, and that her personality was not cut out for having the day-to-day responsibilities of a business owner. She wanted to work on her own but in a more flexible way, and this led her to pursuing her broker/consultant practice.

Expressing: Judy used the mentoring and consulting work she did through the SBA to "kick the tires" on her planned reinvention and to learn everything she needed to learn before making the big commitment.

Connecting: Judy has worked hard to figure out the best ways to get clients and to make her marketing process more efficient and productive. Networking is central to her sales process, and she has effectively used her presence on LinkedIn and other social media to find and convert prospective clients.

DAVID BEADLE

Reframing: David went through a number of reframes in his process, including being willing to participate in the yoga retreat, to transition to a new business completely outside of his area of expertise, and to go to work for the university.

Listening: At a key juncture, David was willing to listen to a friend who helped him see through the confusion he was experiencing and clarify his intention to launch his new business.

Accepting: With all of the heartache that he went through in losing his business and his marriage, David was able to realize that moving forward would require him to let go of the pain and judgment he'd experienced and reengage with life.

Expressing: The expressing step came early for David, using the yoga retreat as the inspiration and the workshop for visualizing what his e-commerce business was going to look like. Subsequently, he used his MA degree program as a forum to iron out the logistical steps necessary to launch the new business.

Connecting: David's network is what kept him going throughout his turnaround and reinvention, from getting the consulting gigs from his former competitor in Bakersfield to connecting to the MA program that would help him launch his business.

MARILYN FRIEDMAN

Reframing: Marilyn's massive reframe was to consider the elementary school position as a viable possibility. She could have rejected it out of hand as being completely off base for her, but she was willing to entertain it and as a result has experienced some unexpected benefits.

Listening: While there were key moments of insight all along the way that Marilyn gained by being open and interactive with friends and colleagues, one big moment was listening to her friend's advice about no longer holding back on submitting her résumé and just generally opening herself back up to the job marketplace.

Accepting: Perhaps the hardest thing for Marilyn to accept was the loss of the long-held job. Even though the CEO of the company told her "you did nothing wrong," it was a challenge for Marilyn to feel good about herself in the aftermath of the layoff. As she has been able to work through the upset, her life has gotten a bit more balanced, and she is able to approach her career with equanimity.

Expressing: Working with her coach was a great opportunity for Marilyn to look at her working options and to identify the deal-breakers that she would just not be willing to accept. The startup position that she ultimately turned down did not fit into her key nonnegotiable criteria, and while it was difficult to turn down a great job, she does not regret that decision for a second.

Connecting: Marilyn is a committed networker who physically sat down with many different people at many different companies both to introduce herself and to see whether there might be a job opening. This networking process worked well for her.

JULIE MURPHY

Reframing: Pivoting to the computer programming course from what might have seemed like an incompatible background in law was a complete reframe for Julie. Later, she was willing to look at a solo career practice as something that was possible for her rather than staying stuck in the belief that she needed to be an employee.

Listening: Relying on family and close friends along the way helped guide Julie and confirm her direction, including seeking out those who were (and are) part of her personal "tribe."

Accepting: Julie came to the understanding that she was the wrong fit for the final two companies she worked for. Then she worked through her fear of becoming a sole practitioner by finding a way to promote her business that was authentic and resonant with who she is.

Expressing: Julie used her mindfulness work and the Search Inside Yourself program as a vehicle or a structure to better understand what she wanted to do, and to concentrate her focus so that, when the timing was right after her daughter graduated from college, she was ready to proceed on her second act.

Connecting: Going to meetups with an incredibly open "attitude of 'yes'" worked well for Julie. She was open to wherever the networking would take her and to discovering opportunities to serve and provide solutions wherever she could.

DAN GOETZ

Reframing: Dan went from seeing himself as a hired gun to being an owner. He also had his epiphany about how to come across in interviews.

Listening: Dan saw the value in the private equity venture even if it didn't align with his values. But it opened him up to figuring out how to do it his way. The Vistage mastermind group input was instrumental in supporting his success in the old company in the new CEO role, and then in helping him lead his new company as a forward-thinking owner/manager.

Accepting: Dan figured out that you can't re-create the old reality of your past. Instead, you have to face forward and step up to the person you have become.

Expressing: Dan had a very proactive approach: create that new reality, draw those pictures, write down your vision. He and his wife mapped out their process, and Dan used his first private equity experience to hone in on what he liked and disliked about the process. The goal was to try it again until he got it right.

Connecting: The Vistage mastermind group was an invaluable forum for Dan to learn new ways of looking at his business. He also relied on his networking practice as his primary job search tool after he was terminated at his company.

VALERIE RAMSEY

Reframing: Valerie was willing to accept the path that was open to her at the resort. Guided by her instinct that Pebble Beach was the right place for her, she was willing to give up the idea of being the concierge and go with the path that was open to her. Had she been focused only on the job itself, she might not have had such a positive experience.

Listening: Looking around and being open to learning what she needed helped Valerie to go out and get the computer skills necessary to advance and then adapt to and pick up the additional skills she needed to get promoted to the executive assistant job.

Accepting: This was particularly important after Valerie's diagnosis and surgery. Whatever her fate or her destiny, she was prepared to accept it and move on, grateful for what she had and the opportunities she had been given.

Expressing: Valerie used her positive outlook to create the path to her job, from focusing on the resort in the first place to following her gut instinct and always looking for how her current opportunity could lead to something more on-target.

Connecting: People skills came very naturally to Valerie. She used her interest in people and in being of service to establish herself in such a way that when the public relations manager job became available, it was a complete no-brainer for her boss to hand it to her.

THREE-MONTH SAMPLE REINVENTION TIMELINE

Three months is a short time to turn any career around, but the agenda that follows illustrates a possible way forward that uses the steps and the strategies in this book to support your Boomer Reinvention process. In your own experience, some things will probably go quickly while others will take much longer. Think of the agenda below as a stepping-off point that you can use to customize your own reinvention timeline.

Week 1

STRATEGY #15—REINVENTION JOURNAL
- Capture random thoughts about current life, work, professional relationships, frustrations, fears, and ideas for work.
- Write at least a page every day or every other day. This is your core reinvention habit, so make it a priority.

STRATEGY #1—ASSESS THE STATUS QUO
- Use Worksheet #1 – Reframing Checklist.
- Create a benchmark for where you are starting your process.
- Focus on the most important things you want to change.

STRATEGY #6—BASIC RESEARCH

- Begin to search on topics and career options that could be of interest. Clip the most valuable or inspiring pieces to your Evernote or OneNote notebooks for future reference.
- Or

STRATEGY #9—BE OF SERVICE

- Start thinking outside yourself, your current thinking, and the circumstances you've been living with. Push your boundaries a little bit, either by doing a deep dive into considering other career options within your field or in a new field, or by signing up to volunteer and be of service to others.

Week 2

STRATEGY #15—REINVENTION JOURNAL

- Keep at this, working to make your journaling as regular and consistent as possible. In the second week, you're probably starting to get the hang of it, but if you're still feeling resistant, back off to twice a week (but commit to doing it!).

STRATEGY #19—TURN YOUR NETWORK INTO A CAREER RELATIONSHIP FUNNEL

- Use the Silver/Gold/Platinum framework to organize your contacts, and think about how you can start leveraging your existing network and activate it.

STRATEGY #20—OPTIMIZE YOUR PROFILE(S)

- Follow the basic steps outlined in the book to bring your LinkedIn profile and other social media profiles up to date and consistent across all platforms.
- Investigate e-books, webinars, and courses you could take to further familiarize yourself with ways to maximize your social media presence.

Week 3

STRATEGY #15—REINVENTION JOURNAL

- Ideas are probably starting to flow a little bit more for you, so capture the top ideas as separate notes in Evernote or OneNote and spend some separate time brainstorming.

STRATEGY #18—MAP YOUR VISION

- Try creating a few mind maps (using any of the three formats) to work with some of the ideas that have come up in your Reinvention Journal.
- To go further with certain specific ideas, you may want to do more Strategy #6—Basic Research to learn more about the ideas.

STRATEGY #19—TURN YOUR NETWORK INTO A CAREER RELATIONSHIP FUNNEL

- Keep working on your contacts. Look for people you already know or have some connection with to set up general meetings to talk about your budding reinvention plans and to get their advice and guidance for possible next steps.

Week 4

STRATEGY #15—REINVENTION JOURNAL

- You should have a pretty steady flow going at this point. If you have hung in there, then journaling is on the verge of becoming an ingrained habit for you—well done!

STRATEGY #7—SOLICIT FEEDBACK

- Set up your interviews with trusted family, friends, colleagues, and advisors, including some of the people you've been in touch with as part of your Strategy #19 from the prior week.

STRATEGY #3—REFRAME LIMITING ROLES, OR, YOU ARE MORE THAN YOUR RÉSUMÉ

- Use **Worksheet #3** to begin reframing your current roles. Use the insights and ideas you have gleaned from your Reinvention Journal and your other activities to inform this process. This will help you to be more open to suggestions that come out of your feedback interviews.

Weeks 5 & 6

STRATEGY #15—REINVENTION JOURNAL

- Keep this going, particularly as you are going to be getting lots of information and feedback from your interviews.

STRATEGY #7—SOLICIT FEEDBACK

- Carry out your interviews over this period, keeping notes and staying open to new ideas. Use **Worksheet #4 to capture the key takeaways from the interviews.**

STRATEGY # 11—STOP BEING A VICTIM

STRATEGY # 13—PRACTICE EMPATHY VS. SYMPATHY

- These two Listening strategies will be helpful to you in your interviews to stay focused, neutral, and open as you receive this valuable information.

STRATEGY #9—BE OF SERVICE

- Continuing to have a service project throughout this process will be a great way of keeping some distance and maintaining perspective on the internal changes that are starting to happen for you.

Weeks 7 & 8

STRATEGY #15—REINVENTION JOURNAL

- Many details may start coming up based on your feedback

interviews. Your journal is a great place to have those internal debates and to explore where your inner guidance is taking you.

STRATEGY #2—REFRAME THE PERSONAL AND THE LOCAL

STRATEGY #4—ACT "AS-IF"

STRATEGY #12—LET YOUR FREAK FLAG FLY

- In the wake of your feedback interviews, you might want to take another look at your comfort zones, habits, and everything that you're used to doing. Use Worksheet #2 to reframe things on the Personal and Local levels.
- Dare to have a little fun with the idea of acting as-if. Keep track of your experiences and discuss them in the Reinvention Journal.
- Also use your Reinvention Journal to bring in the concept from Strategy #12 of reclaiming your identity and planning fun activities to assert the second-act person that you are becoming.

STRATEGY #19—TURN YOUR NETWORK INTO A CAREER RELATIONSHIP FUNNEL

- In the wake of your feedback interviews, continue to engage with your active network and put some of the insights you gained from the interviews into motion. This could be a great opportunity to engage with new people, or to reengage with existing contacts to share a new or emerging direction you want to pursue.

Weeks 9 & 10

STRATEGY #12—LET YOUR FREAK FLAG FLY

STRATEGY #15—REINVENTION JOURNAL

- As you get more involved in the process of narrowing down your reinvention strategy, your journal will start to fill up with ideas that you will want to track separately for how to execute on your vision. Use separate tools, like a spreadsheet, to keep track of these action items.

- Use your journal to continue to deepen your reclaimed identity as you keep building momentum toward your second act.

STRATEGY #17—CONDUCT A SWOT ANALYSIS

STRATEGY #5—REFRAME YOUR MISSION

- You are getting pretty far down the road toward manifesting a viable second-act career choice. Use Worksheet #7 as a guide to conducting your SWOT analysis to make sure that the direction you're going is the right one.
- Create a mission statement as outlined in Strategy #5 to help anchor yourself in the emerging direction and to set positive intentions for your goals.

STRATEGY #10—RECONCILE YOUR RÉSUMÉ

- It's time to clear up any issues on your résumé that may be preventing you from presenting yourself at your best.

STRATEGY #14—CREATE YOUR AFFIRMATION

- Use affirmations to continue to direct positive energy toward your goals and to overcome any tactical obstacles that are causing doubts.

Weeks 11 & 12

STRATEGY #15—REINVENTION JOURNAL

- Use the Reinvention Journal to stay vigilant about any extraneous doubts or obstacles that might be rearing their heads. "Stuff" is always coming up, so use the Journal to observe it; then use your Accepting strategies to handle it.

STRATEGY #16—CREATE A LIVING VISION

- Building on the work you've done with Strategy #6—
  Reframe Your Mission, Strategy #14—Create an Affirmation,
  and Strategy #18—Map Your Vision, use this strategy to
  project yourself one, two, or three years into the future and
  capture what this future is going to feel like.

STRATEGY #21—BECOME A THOUGHT LEADER

- You've done enough work at this point to have developed
  your point of view, and you're ready to start expressing it
  across all of the channels where you are connected. Go for it!

STRATEGY #22—SHINE IN EVERY MEETING

STRATEGY #23—ACE EVERY JOB INTERVIEW

- You're ready to engage positively and proactively beyond
  your Gold and Platinum contacts. You have all the
  preparation at this point to go on job interviews, meet with
  investors, and generally present the completely engaged,
  enthusiastic, value-driven second-act professional that you
  have become.

Weeks 13+

This timeline is a fairly compressed agenda that assumes a basically straight-line progression toward your goals. It's possible that life
will intervene and throw you off course and you'll need additional
time to get back on track. Still, I hope that seeing how the strategies
can work together is helpful in setting your expectations for how a
career reinvention process can unfold.

In the weeks and months ahead, continue to use these strategies
to engage beyond the timeline, particularly the Reinvention Journal,
the Affirmations, and the Living Vision. Continue to solicit feedback
from your trusted group, sharing your progress with them and getting
continued support.